22907793

FOREIGN AID
AND ECONOMIC
DEVELOPMENT
IN THE
MIDDLE EAST

FOREIGN AID AND ECONOMIC DEVELOPMENT IN THE MIDDLE EAST

Egypt, Syria, and Jordan

Victor Lavy
and
Eliezer Sheffer

Foreword by Zvi Sussman

PRAEGER

New York
Westport, Connecticut
London

Library of Congress Cataloging-in-Publication Data

Lavy, Victor.
  Foreign aid and economic development in the Middle East : Egypt,
Syria, and Jordan / Victor Lavy and Eliezer Sheffer ; foreword by
Zvi Sussman.
    p. cm.
  Includes bibliographical references and index.
  ISBN 0-275-93827-1 (alk. paper)
    1. Egypt—Economic conditions—1952-   2. Egypt—Economic policy.
  3. Egypt—Defenses—Economic aspects.   4. Syria—Economic
  conditions—1918-   5. Syria—Economic policy.   6. Syria—Defenses—
  Economic aspects.   7. Jordan—Economic conditions.   8. Jordan—
  Economic policy.   9. Jordan—Defenses—Economic aspects.
  10. Economic assistance—Arab countries.   11. f-ua a-sy a-jo.
  I. Sheffer, Eliezer. II. Title.
  HC830.L38   1991
  338.9'11'0956—dc20   90-27796

British Library Cataloguing in Publication Data is available.

Copyright © 1991 by Victor Lavy and Eliezer Sheffer

Library of Congress Catalog Card Number: 90-27796
ISBN: 0-275-93827-1

First published in 1991

Praeger Publishers, One Madison Avenue, New York, NY   10010
An imprint of Greenwood Publishing Group, Inc.

Printed in the United States of America

The paper used in this book complies with the
Permanent Paper Standard issued by the National
Information Standards Organization (Z39.48-1984).

10 9 8 7 6 5 4 3 2 1

CONTENTS

Part III: Outlook for Reform and Adjustment

FOREWORD

This study deals with the resumption of economic growth in the Middle East. It examines the decline from prosperity to stagnation in Egypt, Syria, and Jordan during the 1980s, the long-term constraints on the renewal of growth, and in particular, the defense burden, the role of foreign aid and domestic savings in achieving sustained growth, the required policy reforms and structural changes, and the scope of regional economic cooperation. The study is the first for the research program of the Israeli International Institute for Applied Economic Policy Review on economic means to promote and enhance peace in the region.

Zvi Sussman
Director of Research
Israeli International Institute
    for Applied Economic Policy
Review

ACKNOWLEDGMENTS

This study was sponsored by the Israeli International Institute for Applied Economic Policy Review. We owe much to its research director, Zvi Sussman, who suggested this study to us and provided critical and useful comments on earlier drafts.

We would like to thank participants in the three special workshops held at the Israeli International Institute during which various chapters of the book were presented and discussed. These discussions led to significant improvements in the manuscript. Excellent research assistance was provided at various stages by Jacob Ben Moshe.

We are very grateful to Nancy Webber for typing and retyping the numerous drafts of the chapters. Bruce Ross-Larson deserves gratitude for allowing us to draw on his editorial skills in putting it all together.

INTRODUCTION

Iraq's invasion of Kuwait on August 2, 1990 and the fallout from the Gulf war are having dramatic political, military, and economic effects on the entire Middle East. There still is much uncertainty about the long-term outcome of the crisis. What will be the new balance of power in the Persian Gulf? What will be the political and economic ramifications for Egypt, Syria, and Jordan? There is uncertainty, too, about how long the crisis will continue—and where oil prices will settle.

Our research focus in this book is on the negative effects of large (and largely transitory) capital flows to Egypt, Syria, and Jordan, capital wasted because of inappropriate adjustments. We describe and analyze the external and internal factors that led all three economies from prosperity in the decade of the 1970s to a deep and continuing crisis in the 1980s. Throughout, we emphasize the negative economic consequences of large military and defense expenditures, price and resource allocation distortions, and malfunctioning economic systems. An appropriate adjustment would have been macroeconomic policies to build modern production infrastructure and create a system of financial intermediation to channel resources to the most productive investments. The new reality expected in the Middle East region after the Gulf crisis does not change the author's opinion about the reforms, structural changes, and external resources needed for long-run and sustained economic recovery. The Gulf war will nevertheless have the effect of slowing the economic recovery in Egypt, Syria, and Jordan. All past military confrontations in the Middle East have escalated the arms race in the region and hampered development and economic growth. Increases in military expenditures have already taken place, but it is not clear whether they will remain high. Higher permanent defense budgets will add to the resource constraints in the region. They will not only require more drastic economic recovery policies, but also reduce the chance of these policies to achieve success. There is no easy way out from the economic crisis of Egypt, Syria, and Jordan. The prospects of a transitory increase in the flow of foreign exchange from aid, higher oil prices, and forgiven external debt are not going to solve the structural and fundamental problems of these economies. With today's uncertainty, estimates of future levels of aid flows and other sources of foreign exchange receipts have no meaning. Aid can compensate somewhat for the direct and indirect losses Egypt, Syria, and Jordan sustained in the Gulf war: the loss of remittances to the Egyptian economy from workers who fled Iraq, the massive influx of refugees into Jordan, the cut in Saudi oil and oil transfers to Jordan, or the losses to Jordan's income because of the economic embargo on Iraq.

In addition, Egypt (as a big exporter) and Syria (to less extent) did benefit from higher oil prices. All these short-term effects are small, however, compared with the structural long-term problems. Foreign aid, because it is erratic, should not be relied on in the long run to deal with these problems. The events of the last two decades in Egypt, Syria, and Jordan support this argument. The only path these countries have is through responsible economic programs and policies, however painful they may be during the adjustment period.

I
FROM
PROSPERITY TO
DECLINE

1

INAPPROPRIATE POLICY RESPONSES TO INFLOWS OF FOREIGN FUNDS

Worse off today than they were before the oil boom, Egypt, Syria, and Jordan show that foreign aid—if improperly used—can weaken rather than strengthen an economy.

Egypt, Syria, and Jordan provide the economic equivalent of a laboratory setting for studying what an economy shouldn't do with an abundance of foreign funds. Like the heirs who party rather than develop a career, they failed to use it prudently in ways that would create an earning potential for future meager years. Foreign capital alone—however massive in quantity—cannot produce economic miracles. It can even exacerbate poor economic performance through disincentives to reform and negative effects on the economy's structure. For example, Egypt is second only to Israel in the amount of foreign aid it received, yet it has the most severe external debt problem in the world—worse in relative terms than that of Brazil and Argentina.

The three countries' economies share certain features—all three, for example, have engaged in decades of military build-up. But they differ greatly in economic and political structure and ideology. Syria is a fully socialist state, its economy modeled on Eastern European economies. Egypt is a semicentrally planned socialist economy. Jordan has an almost completely free capitalist, or market-oriented, economy. Despite these differences, the three countries experienced almost identical external shocks in the 1970s and 1980s. The result was the same in all three countries: deep economic crises, heavy external debts, and severe balance of payments problems.

This book is not about the Middle East conflict. Instead it is a study of economic developments and policy responses in Egypt, Syria, and Jordan during the boom years of foreign capital inflows and the period of their decline. It is an analysis of how foreign aid can help—or limit—economic development. Drawing on the experiences of these three Middle Eastern countries, we hope to clarify the lessons policymakers should draw about the changes developing countries everywhere must make to move from stagnation to sustained growth. In analyzing what happened during the period of prosperity and the transition to a period of austerity, we pay specific attention to the short-term and long-term crises in the three countries and to the effect of the military buildup on their economies.

WHAT EGYPT, SYRIA, AND JORDAN HAVE IN COMMON

All three economies are poor. Per capita gross national product (GNP) in Egypt was less than $700 in 1987, and about $1,600 in Syria and Jordan. With a GNP of less than $5 billion, Jordan's was the smallest economy. Syria's GNP in 1987 was $18 billion in 1987, Egypt's $35 billion. All three countries have high population growth rates, ranging from 2.7 to 3.7 percent annually. Egypt's population reached more than 50 million in 1987, Syria's 11 million, and Jordan's 2.8 million. The ratio of population to resources is least favorable in Egypt.

In many important characteristics—in their economic and political systems, natural resources, income levels, and labor skills—the three countries differ greatly. Reviewing them as a single regional group is justified because of the features and recent economic trends they share.

In particular, their economies are all significantly affected by booms and slumps in the neighboring oil-rich states—and all are suffering from the current oil slump.

None of them is a major net oil exporter. Jordan does not produce oil, and Syria became a net oil exporter only in 1987. Of the three, only Egypt can be considered a medium-sized net exporter of oils: it has thus been affected directly by the rise and fall in oil prices.[1] But all three countries benefit from oil prosperity. They benefit from workers' remittances from the oil-rich states, from which Syria and Jordan also receive large official financial transfers. Official Arab aid to Egypt ceased in 1979, after the signing of the peace treaty with Israel (but was replaced by U.S. aid). This heavy flow of funds from the oil-exporting countries has exposed the economies of Egypt, Syria, and Jordan to the indirect effect of fluctuations in oil earnings. With the downturn in oil after 1981, they began to accumulate foreign debt rapidly. The servicing burden of this debt has become intolerable and poses extremely difficult problems for all three countries, despite newly agreed-on rescheduling arrangements.

In addition, all three countries have huge military expenditures. They are on the front line in recurrent wars and in a prolonged conflict with Israel. For more than four decades, immense domestic resources have been allocated to support a buildup of military strength. These national efforts have been supported by military aid in the form of large grants or loans to finance arms imports. As a result, these countries have the highest defense-to-GNP ratios in the world. Egypt spent 18 percent of its GNP on armaments in 1972, Jordan spent as much as 20 percent in recent years, and military spending in Syria (and Israel) reached 25 percent of GNP in the early 1980s.

$110 BILLION IN CAPITAL FLOWS—AND $42 BILLION IN WORKER'S REMITTANCES

When a country's economic structures and institutions are weak, foreign capital can aggravate poor economic performance by creating disincentives to reform. Prices become more distorted, and public spending on subsidies, defense, and low-return investment projects more inflated. If appropriate policy measures are not implemented, heavy capital flows from abroad can also distort resource allocation, weaken the balance of payments, and perpetuate a dependence on foreign aid.

Flows of capital to Egypt, Syria, Jordan, and Israel were enormous—totaling approximately $110 billion—in the decade from 1978 to 1987 (table 1.1). Foreign funds for Egypt and Israel came largely from the United States, as military and civilian aid. Syria and Jordan received most foreign capital as aid from the Arab oil-exporting countries. The three Arab states also borrowed development funds from the World Bank.[2] And they borrowed in world financial markets as well. About half the $110 billion total—an average of more than $5 billion a year—financed arms imports. The remaining $55 billion generally supported the balance of payments.[3] Little was used to diversify exports, to accelerate the modernization of agriculture and industry, or in other ways to reduce gradually the dependence on foreign aid.

The three Arab countries have also benefited from workers' remittances, which totaled $42 billion over the decade.[4] These remittances can be seen as a form of capital imports since they require neither technological progress nor domestic export projects. Their structural impact on an economy resembles that of capital inflows rather than ordinary export expansion. Workers' remittances are usually classified as private current transfers.[5] Between 1978 and 1987, workers' remittances to Egypt, Syria, and Jordan contributed more than twice as much as total non-oil exports to foreign exchange earnings. Unlike official transfers and most long-term loans—channeled directly to government—workers' remittances are private receipts. As such, they contribute to the growth in private consumption, construction, accumulation of financial assets, and investment in business.

A medium-sized net oil exporter, Egypt also experiences substantial windfall gains when oil prices rise, and its Suez Canal dues could also be seen as a form of rent income. Oil and Suez Canal earnings accounted for 20 percent of Egypt's gross domestic product in the early 1980s, but less than half a percent of total employment. This share in GDP dropped to half its peak when oil prices fell. Again, only a fraction of foreign exchange earnings went to productive use for accelerating long-term growth.

THE FAILURE TO ADJUST EARLY

Absorbing massive amounts of external capital presents problems and benefits. By augmenting available resources, abundant foreign exchange funds loosen the constraints on growth and contribute to the expansion of employment, consumption, and public services. Offsetting these gains are negative side-effects that are particularly common when the influx of funds is only temporary, as in Egypt, Syria, and Jordan. These side-effects include an appreciating currency and a rising demand for imports. The ultimate effect of capital inflows depends largely on the policy responses and adjustment measures adopted as the flow of foreign funds rises and falls.[6]

Increased government revenue from foreign sources also encourages increased military and civilian public spending. To suppress inflation when domestic demand is excessive, governments offer more subsidies on food and other basic products, and subsidize export promotion. But subsidies of food and public utilities are hard to reverse, as Egypt and Jordan have learned—and governments that begin spending freely have trouble breaking the habit. When foreign resources are abundant, governments tend to want to spend a lot fast—often overinvesting in large-scale, low-return projects that are difficult to abandon when economic conditions change. Many decisions during boom years are hard to reverse when economic conditions change. Reluctant to take the necessary painful measures, they borrow abroad to finance the continuation of their economic policies. Such borrowing is not, however, an appropriate substitute for adjusting to changing circumstances.

The adjustment costs of a decline in foreign income can be considerable, and inappropriate policy responses can aggravate economic contraction. Balance of payments crises and the need to rapidly cut fiscal deficits often lead to major devaluations, sharply reduced subsidies, and tighter import controls—all aimed at restoring equilibrium. Such measures can also cause prolonged stagflation, however. And borrowing abroad, rather than increasing domestic savings, eventually produces the kind of debt crises that Egypt, Syria, and Jordan are experiencing. Ultimately, borrowing abroad increases a country's dependence on external factors and its vulnerability to external shocks.

The decade of abundant foreign exchange resources and accelerated growth in Egypt, Syria, and Jordan ended in the early 1980s. Falling oil prices and oil export volumes eroded the export earnings of Egypt and the Gulf oil states.[7] Official aid transfers from the Arab oil states to Syria and Jordan were cut to half their peak during 1979-1981. As economic development and activity in the oil states declined, workers' remittances to Egypt, Syria, and Jordan first stabilized in the mid-1980s and then declined. All three countries now face a shortage of foreign exchange.[8] At first, they continued to borrow heavily from abroad. Later—after foreign credits dried up—they implemented more drastic stabilization policies to maintain macroeconomic equilibrium.

These stabilization policies have probably had a negative impact on economic performance. Between 1986 and 1989, when the debt crisis deteriorated and arrears mounted, all three countries had to cut merchandise imports significantly through direct controls and restrictive domestic policies. They also cut subsidies and raised prices for utilities and public sector enterprises. And to reduce their vast fiscal deficits to more manageable proportions, they also cut current and capital public spending. Tables 1.2 and 1.3 show the declining trend in public consumption (including military spending) and investment ratios (which decline as public investments decline). Table 1.4 illustrates the slowdown and decline in private consumption. (Also see figure 1.1.)

Egypt, Syria, and Jordan have also significantly devalued their currencies in recent years. They took this step only after it was made a condition for International Monetary Fund (IMF) support of stabilization programs Egypt and Jordan had requested. (IMF support was crucial for debt-rescheduling agreements with Egypt's and Jordan's creditors.) The IMF also required that they remove subsidies, adjust controlled prices, cut budget deficits, and establish restrictive monetary policies.

Adjusting to the shortage of foreign exchange has been painful for the three Arab countries. Relaxing controls on inflation caused prices to rise, which led to widespread popular unrest, most dramatic in the April 1989 food riots in Jordan. In Syria, a strong centralized regime prevented riots despite the rise in inflation from 1986 to 1988, the sharp erosion in real wages, and the steep decline in both private and public consumption.[9] In Egypt, the decline in private and public consumption has been more gradual.

In brief, the outcome of a temporary large-scale influx of funds from abroad, partly as loans, can be a painful adjustment when those funds are reduced. Egypt, Syria, and Jordan are now experiencing economic stagnation because the heavy flow of external capital was shut off and adjustment responses to the new economic conditions further reduced economic activity. All three countries have become heavily indebted, undermining their capacity to accelerate economic growth because resources that otherwise could have been used for development must be used for debt service. And because of the debt crises, foreign private creditors shut off their lending to the three countries in 1987.[10]

Structural changes in boom years—inflating the nontradable sectors—are especially hard to reverse. It takes prolonged efforts to achieve fiscal balance, higher domestic savings, a reduced public sector, realistic exchange rates, and the removal of price distortions, which also hurt the tradable sector. The governments of Egypt and Jordan now seem to recognize that military spending must be cut to ensure the success of their stabilization and adjustment efforts. Officials in both countries have recently acknowledged that heavy defense spending is contributing to their economic difficulties.

MORE APPROPRIATE RESPONSES

It is difficult to justify the build-up of enormous foreign debts on top of massive one-way transfers of foreign exchange in Egypt, Syria, and Jordan—all of which have highly centralized systems for determining the uses of official aid, net capital imports, and, in Egypt's case, windfall profits from oil. What should these countries have done differently to benefit more from the glut in foreign exchange and to minimize adjustment costs in the contractionary phase of the cycle? The three countries may not have been able to avoid some of the drawbacks of large transfers and net capital inflows. But they could have minimized their disadvantages by reducing price-distorting practices, by relying more on market forces and efficiency considerations, and by pursuing more determined anticyclical stabilization policies.

Debt, stagflation, balance of payments crises, and the declining per capita income and consumption in the three Arab countries show how gains from capital inflows can later be lost through adjustment. Appropriate policy responses must be made throughout the cycle if a temporary influx of foreign exchange is to benefit the economy. Inappropriate responses during boom periods and careless adjustment measures during economic downturns are both likely to accentuate economic difficulties. The macroeconomic adjustments to rising and falling inflows tend to be asymmetrical, and it is hard to reverse the structural changes that result.

In Egypt, Syria, and Jordan, a more determined policy to limit the inflationary impact of rapidly expanding public spending could have softened the subsequent downturn. Saving more and spending less in the public sector would have produced more domestic balance, less foreign debt, and fewer debt-service obligations. More restrained external borrowing by the private and public sectors could have held domestic demand down to more desirable levels during the boom.

Instead, much of the capital inflow went for fast-absorbing large-scale projects, rather than being used to diversify and modernize the economy and to reduce its vulnerability to external shocks. True, some price must be paid for a sharp rise and fall in the flow of foreign funds. But more appropriate policy responses could have increased the gains from extra foreign resources and could have minimized some of the adjustment costs when they began to decline. Investments should have been evaluated in terms of whether and how much they would contribute to long-term economic growth. The recent deep recession shows that a framework for sustained growth has not yet been developed.

PLAN OF THIS BOOK

In Part I we analyze the changes between the period of prosperity (roughly 1973 through the early 1980s) and the crisis and decline of the rest of the 1980s. We emphasize the pattern of unbalanced growth and the bias toward nontradable sectors brought on by the huge inflow of foreign resources. We show that distorted economic policy and an overactive public sector were the main causes of maladjustment and poor economic performance. Variations in the three countries' economic philosophy and ideology are shown as factors in their differing reactions to similar changes in the economic environment. We refer to the debt overhangs that pose extremely difficult economic problems, particularly for Egypt and Jordan.

In Part II we move from a focus on short-term considerations to an analysis of long-term constraints on growth—not only the constraints of human and physical capital, but the uniquely heavy, 40-year military burden. With the highest ratios of military spending to gross national product, the three countries have devoted immense human, material, and national energies that could have been channeled to social and economic development.

In Part III we recommend policy reform and structural changes to sustain the region's economic growth and socioeconomic development. We emphasize that foreign aid will be needed to support such reforms and adjustment, and we estimate what will be needed to bridge expected resource gaps.

NOTES

1. Syria's net oil exports amounted to $210 million in 1987 and $385 million in 1988. Earlier net oil exports were negligible. Egypt exported $1,220 million crude and oil products in 1986-1987, down from $2,640 million in 1983-1984.

2. Egypt's outstanding debt to the World Bank and the International Development Association (IDA) increased $2,340 million between 1978 and 1987. During the same period, Syria's increased $430 million and Jordan's $460 million. (World Bank 1987b.)

3. It should be noted that the item "official capital grants" to Syria and Jordan from the oil states have declined since 1982. See table 2.3.

4. See also table 2.2. After rising sharply for a decade, workers' remittances began to decline slightly in 1985.

5. See for example World Bank 1989e.

6. Alan Gelb (1988) elaborates on the problems of absorbing oil windfalls and the appropriate adjustments needed when oil earnings decline.

7. Saudi Arabia's oil exports shrank from a peak of $111 billion in 1981 to $26 billion in 1985, $18 billion in 1986, and $20 billion in 1987 and 1988.

8. An escalating debt-service burden has aggravated the foreign exchange shortage. See chapter 2 and table 2.7.

9. See tables 1.2 and 1.4 and figure 1.1. The retail price index in Damascus increased an average 41 percent a year in 1986-1988, compared with an average 10.8 percent a year in 1983-1985 (Syria, Central Bureau of Statistics, 198x).

10. In 1987, the capital account turned negative on Egypt's and Syria's balance of payment ledgers: amortization exceeded new borrowing.

Table 1.1 Total Net Capital Inflows, 1978-1987
($US billions)

Country	Recorded official transfers (1)	Other recorded long-term net loans[a] (2)	Military grants and loans[b] (3)	Total[c] (4)	Workers' remittances (5)
Egypt	6.5[d]	26.1	—	32.6	28.0
Syria	12.2	2.2	10.0	24.4	5.0[e]
Jordan	8.5	2.9	4.0	15.4	8.5
Subtotal	27.5	31.2	14.0	72.4	41.5
Israel	25.0	11.0	—	36.0	*
Total	52.2	42.2	14.0	108.4	

a. Increase in public/publicly guaranteed long-term outstanding external debt between the end of 1977 and the end of 1987. Probably understated for Syria and Jordan.
b. Own rough estimate of unrecorded military grants and loans to finance arms imports.
c. Does not include foreign direct investments, which are substantial only in Egypt, particularly in the oil sector.
d. Aid to finance arms imports is not included.
e. Partial record. See footnote to table 2.2.
* Net outflow of workers' remittances to the administered territories.
Source: World Bank 1989e and IMF data. Column 3, own estimate.

Table 1.2 Growth in Government Consumption, Annual Real Growth Rates
(percentages)

	1973-81	1982-87	1985	1986	1987
Egypt	6.7ᵃ	3.0	1.3	0.7	-2.3
Jordan	8.1	5.0	4.4	11.0	2.7
Syria	14.0	-2.7	-7.5	-10.1	-15.4

a. For 1975-1981.
Source: World Bank 1989e.

Table 1.3 Investment Ratios, Gross Domestic Investment as a Percentage of GDP

Year	Egypt	Syria	Jordan
1970	13.9	13.7	12.8
1971	13.2	14.8	19.1
1972	12.3	20.1	20.6
1973	13.1	12.4	18.0
1974	22.5	24.8	26.5
1975	33.4	25.0	28.5
1976	28.4	31.4	35.6
1977	29.2	35.5	39.4
1978	31.7	27.4	35.3
1979	32.8	26.2	37.2
1980	27.5	27.5	41.1
1981	29.5	23.2	50.5
1982	30.1	23.7	46.9
1983	28.7	23.6	35.9
1984	27.5	23.7	32.4
1985	26.7	23.8	30.5
1986	23.7	23.3	29.6
1987	19.3	18.6	26.4
1988	20.1	16.6	23.7

Years	Average ratios		
	Egypt	Syria	Jordan
1970-73	13.1	15.3	17.6
1975-79	31.1	29.6[a]	46.2[b]
1984-88	23.5	21.2	28.5

a. For 1976-1980.
b. For 1980-1982.
Source: World Bank 1989e. World Bank 1989b.

Table 1.4 Growth in Private Consumption, Annual Real Growth Rates, 1973-1987
(percentages)

	Total			Per capita		
	Egypt	Syria	Jordan	Egypt	Syria	Jordan
1973-1981	7.1ᵃ	13.3	7.0	4.3ᵃ	9.4	4.5
1982-1987	5.0	-3.4	4.1	2.2	-6.8	0.4
1982	6.3	-8.4	14.0	3.3	-11.5	10.1
1983	4.0	4.2	10.5	1.2	-0.7	6.5
1984	7.5	-9.8	3.2	4.7	-12.9	-0.5
1985	6.7	5.8	0.3	4.0	2.2	-3.2
1986	3.0	-4.6	1.8	0.4	-8.0	-1.5
1987	2.3	-6.5	-4.3	-0.1	-9.8	-7.9
1988*	1.7	—	-2.3	-1.0	—	-5.9

a. For 1975-1981.
* Preliminary figures.
Source: World Bank 1989e. For Jordan 1988, Ministry of Planning (cited in IMF data). For Egypt 1988, World Bank 1989b.

Table 1.5 Indices of Private Per Capita Consumption
(in constant prices; 1980 = 100)

Year	Egypt	Syria	Jordan
1974	73.5	75.4	62.3
1975	65.8	87.6	69.4
1976	66.3	88.1	74.8
1977	77.7	84.6	82.8
1978	78.8	91.9	90.1
1979	91.7	93.8	103.5
1980	100.0	100.0	100.0
1981	98.6	121.4	104.1
1982	101.9	107.5	114.8
1983	103.1	108.2	122.3
1984	107.9	94.3	121.4
1985	112.3	96.3	116.3
1986	112.7	88.6	114.8
1987	112.6	79.9	105.9
1988	111.5	—	99.7

Source: World Bank 1989e. World Bank 1989b.

2
FROM BOOM— TO DECLINE

In the early 1980s a sharp reversal of the unprecedented prosperity of the 1970s propelled Egypt, Jordan, and Syria into deep economic crises. The main sources of income from the boom years—oil exports, aid, and remittances—dried up with the leveling and later collapse of oil prices. Desperate, the three countries turned to foreign lenders to try to perpetuate their spending patterns from the boom years, driving their balance of payments deficits and stocks of external debt to tremendous highs. And when it became apparent that the boom years were not soon returning, the three countries lay vulnerable to their rapid population growth, heavy military spending, and deficient economic policies—all tolerable during the boom years, but each untenable after them. Their economies stopped growing, and in some years contracted. And their per capita incomes, after soaring in the 1970s, began to fall.

THE BOOM

For the decade beginning in 1973—years of higher inflation, higher unemployment, growing balance of payments dificulties, and economic decline for most of the world—growth took off in the Middle East, especially in the major oil-producing countries but also in Egypt, Syria, and Jordan (table 2.1). Income from oil exports in the Persian Gulf countries jumped from $4 billion a year in 1970 to a peak of $180 billion a year in 1980-1981. The windfall from the high oil prices in the 1970s brought great wealth to the oil-producing countries—wealth that radiated to the poorer countries of the region through generous financial assistance, through remittances from workers who migrated to the richer states, and to some extent through trade. Between 1973 and 1981, growth hit record levels in Egypt, Syria, and Jordan, and their per capita incomes rose dramatically, reaching in 1987 $670 in Egypt, $1,640 in Syria, and $1,560 in Jordan (see figure 2.1).[1] With this prosperity, domestic absorption grew faster than the GDP. The gap was financed by foreign aid, workers' remittances from abroad, and external loans.

At the same time that the oil-rich countries were providing income from workers' remittances, they also increased their financial aid to—and their demand for goods from—Egypt, Syria, and Jordan. The entire region was blanketed with roads, airports, seaports, water systems, communication networks, and electricity generation and transmission facilities—and with hundereds of thousands of dwelling units and many schools, hospitals, and other public buildings. Public services were extended, industrial plants built, and new economic activities developed in the oil states. So the influence of the Middle East's growth in oil revenues spread beyond the borders of the oil-producing countries, accelerating economic growth and structural change in Egypt, Syria, and Jordan.

Workers' remittances

Among the external circumstances that helped accelerate the growth process, workers' remittances were a major—if not the major—factor. Because the high-income oil countries are thinly populated, they could not meet the increased manpower needs for construction projects or for the new plants and services. To meet this demand, millions of workers from the poor countries of the Middle East began pouring into the rich oil-producing countries, in a process that had far-reaching implications for the entire Middle Eastern economy. Within a few years workers' remittances from abroad would become a major source of foreign currency income in Egypt, Syria, and Jordan. The large-scale export of workers would help finance the increased imports needed for accelerated economic growth, as well as reduce unemployment in the exporting countries.

A trickle before 1974, the flow of foreign workers to the oil-producing countries of the Persian Gulf increased rapidly in 1974-1975 and continued climbing for 10 years.[2] The flow peaked at about 5 million workers in 1983-1984,[3] with about half of them in Saudia Arabia. More than 60 percent of the workers in Saudi Arabia were foreign, as were about 80 percent in Kuwait and about 85 percent in Qatar and the United Arab Emirates.[4] About two-thirds of the foreign workers were from neighboring Arab countries; the other third mainly from India, Pakistan, and the Far East. More than half the foreign Arab workers in the oil-producing Gulf countries came from Egypt, with the rest mainly from Syria, Jordan, Lebanon, the Yemen Arab Republic (YAR), and the People's Democratic Republic of Yemen.

Not surprisingly, then, exports of workers' services were the main source of foreign exchange earnings in Egypt, Syria, and Jordan during the 1970s. Jordan in particular relied on income from workers' remittances—exporting the equivalent of half its domestic labor force.[5]

Egypt and Syria exported close to 15 percent of their labor force. In the early 1980s, remittances transferred by the roughly 2 million Egyptian workers abroad totaled about $3.5 billion a year. Remittances from 400,000 Syrian workers reached about $1 billion a year, and those from roughly 330,000 Jordanian workers came to about $1.25 billion a year. Compared with the negligible remittances before 1975 (table 2.2), these figures are nothing short of astonishing.

Workers' remittances have thus been an important source of hard currency for these three countries—especially for Jordan, which has the smallest economy. In 1984 the flow of remittances to Jordan reached more than a quarter of its GNP. Net transfers (after subtracting remittances from foreign workers in Jordan to other countries) reached 20 percent of GNP and 170 percent of exports of goods in 1982-1984.

In Egypt workers' remittances in 1982-1984 reached about 10 percent of GNP—three times its merchandise exports, excluding oil. In Syria the remittances for this period were about 6 percent of GNP—roughly twice its earnings from exports.

Aid

The oil-producing countries had given little financial aid before 1973, but with the region's increased wealth after 1973, the poorer Arab countries began demanding more foreign assistance. Egypt, Syria, and Jordan got most of the aid until the signing of the peace treaty between Egypt and Israel in 1978—after which Arab aid to Egypt ended (and generous economic and military aid from the United States began). In the same year, Arab aid to Syria and Jordan increased as a result of the resolutions of the Baghdad Conference—which included pledges of aid totaling $30 billion over 10 years to the "confrontation" countries that rejected peace with Israel.

Most official unilateral transfers to Syria and Jordan are Arab aid, so aid flows to them mirror the economic situation of the oil-rich countries. Reaching their peak in 1979-1981, official transfers to Jordan and Syria were large in relation to their economies—31 percent of GNP in Jordan, 11 percent in Syria, and almost a third of total imports of goods and services in the two countries (table 2.3).[6] Also at the peaks these transfers reached 64 percent of total exports of goods and services in Syria and exceeded by 9 percent the exports of goods and services in Jordan.[7] For these two countries, the receipts from official transfers were even greater than the receipts from workers' remittances in the early 1980s.

Trade

As a medium-sized oil exporter, Egypt also benefited directly from higher oil prices. Oil became a principal export from Egypt, netting $2,640 million in the peak year 1983-1984 as compared to only $135 million in 1974. Syria's foreign trade balance in oil and oil products was not significantly positive until 1986. Before then, it imported about the same amount of oil as it exported. Since the discovery in the center of Syria's northern region of the new Thayem oil field—which began to produce high-quality oil in mid-1986—Syria has become a small net exporter of oil and oil products. In 1988 Syria's net oil exports reached $385 million, comparable to 57 percent of nonfuel merchandise exports.[8]

Shortages of foreign currency had previously constrained development in Egypt, in Syria, and to a lesser extent in Jordan, and periodic balance of payments crises had limited domestic economic activity. Abundant foreign currency during the boom allowed annual growth of the GDP to accelerate to almost 9 percent in Egypt and Syria and to nearly 11 percent in Jordan (table 2.1), high rates compared both with other economies and with earlier periods. (But because of rapid population growth, per capita GDP grew only 5 to 6 percent a year in Egypt and Syria and 8 percent a year in Jordan.) These years of prosperity brought increasing investments and public consumption and a higher standard of living (see tables 1.2 to 1.4). Imports increased rapidly, financed by the new sources of foreign currency income. Public spending increased in all three countries, and since many of the new foreign currency receipts went directly to the treasury, the governments could avoid raising taxes.

The increased availability of foreign exchange contributed much to economic growth during this period (table 2.4). Industrial and agricultural exports had previously been the major source of foreign exchange, but during the boom they were stagnant. From 1972 to 1982 the real income from traditional exports grew only very slowly (Syria and Jordan) or even fell (Egypt). Income from other new sources, however, rose sharply—from $400 million to about $7.4 billion in Egypt, and from negligible sums to $1.8 in Syria and to about $2 billion in Jordan (table 2.4). This remarkable rise financed the steep growth in imports during the boom.

THE DECLINE

In 1982 the economic situation of the oil-rich Gulf began to deteriorate.[9] Declining oil consumption and an increase in oil production from non-OPEC sources held oil prices down—leading to their later collapse in 1986—and oil exports continued to decline. Income from oil exports by the Gulf states fell from a peak of $180 billion a year in 1980-1981 to about $60 billion a year in 1986-1987.

The drop in income was most striking in Saudi Arabia, the main oil producer: from $110 billion in 1981 to $18 billion in 1986 and $20 billion in 1987. The ramifications of this huge drop in Saudi income were especially far-reaching, since it was the largest provider of financial aid to the confrontation states and the largest importer of foreign labor.[10] The drop in income opened a large deficit in Saudi Arabia's current balance of payments, which called for reduced government spending, investments, and imports. It also meant a decrease in foreign aid to Syria and Jordan (table 2.3).[11]

The number of foreign workers in the oil-producing countries leveled off and then declined, reducing what workers' remittances contributed to the balance of payments in Egypt, Syria, and Jordan (table 2.2). Egypt also lost income from declining oil revenues—going from $2.6 billion in 1983-1984 to $1.2 billion in 1986-1987—and from a slowdown in the growth of Suez Canal dues.[12]

Domestic inflationary pressures during the boom in Egypt, Syria, and Jordan were largely offset by the growth of imports, but the decline in foreign currency inflows after 1982 took away this way of suppressing inflation. So, to reduce aggregate demand (including imports), the governments of all three countries were forced to restrict government spending. They also applied direct controls on imports to cope with balance of payments difficulties. As a result of stabilization measures and the drop in export earnings, economic growth fell sharply or turned negative. Per capita GDP fell 4.5 percent a year in Syria between 1982 and 1987, and in Jordan it increased only 0.1 percent a year (table 2.5). In Egypt per capita GDP continued to grow until 1985, but stagnated in 1986-1987 and declined in 1988-1989.

Rising vulnerability

By the early 1980s exports from traditional sectors in all three countries had become a minor source of foreign exchange. Increased domestic demand for agricultural and industrial products and overvalued exchange rates had made exports less profitable. As a result, Egypt, Syria, and Jordan were overly dependent on unstable external sources of foreign exchange—the consequences of which became apparent in 1982, when oil prices declined, the oil economies contracted, and workers abroad had to come home.

The economies of the three countries deteriorated quickly because of their unbalanced growth during the decade of prosperity. The relative abundance of foreign currency from special sources made it possible for their economies to expand in such nontradable sectors as services and construction—which grew to occupy a disproportionate share of the national economies and to be subject to the "Dutch disease" of expanding nontradables at the expense of exports. Previously, imports by the three countries had increased only as the result of efforts to expand tourism and their exports of agricultural and industrial products. The influx of huge amounts of external aid, workers' remittances, and other special income (such as that from Suez Canal dues and oil exports in Egypt) diminished the felt need to develop export production. (Chapters 3 through 6 discuss structural and other changes from the massive inflow of foreign exchange.)

Current and capital public spending expanded rapidly during the boom in Egypt, Syria, and Jordan, because of the flow of foreign currency receipts into the public treasury and the general feeling of prosperity. Between 1973 and 1981, for example, real public consumption grew an average 6.7 percent a year in Egypt, 8 percent in Jordan, and 14 percent in Syria (table 1.2). The resulting budget deficits[13] were financed by external borrowing and internal loans from banks and the public, which in turn increased the external deficit. The multiple exchange rates in Egypt and Syria (analyzed in the next chapter) aggravated the problem by encouraging imports and discouraging exports.

Egypt, Syria, and Jordan failed to take advantage of the boom to reduce their vulnerability to external shocks. Essential reforms aimed at removing distortions and implementing structural change—conditions essential for sustained economic growth—would have been easy when foreign currency was abundant. But the three countries did not develop or expand technological bases or other conditions essential for developing new exports and economic independence. Instead, pervasive systems of price control, distorted allocations of resources, unrealistic exchange rates, and the lack of proper incentives prevented the development of a large, diversified export sector.

Short-sighted government policies—probably based on the misconception that external conditions would be favorable for a long time—thus contributed to the economic stagnation and decline of Egypt, Syria, and Jordan in the 1980s. The inflated public spending in the 1970s and early 1980s had created large budget deficits, intensified inflationary pressures, and undermined the balance of payments when economic conditions worsened. And the use of foreign loans to finance the current account deficit boosted external debts, the servicing burden for which was already high.

Falling remittances, aid, and trade

The leveling and subsequent decline of foreign currency income from foreign aid, workers' remittances, and oil exports severely destabilized the balance of payments and forced the governments of Egypt, Syria, and Jordan to take drastic measures to reduce domestic demand and limit imports. The unavoidable result was repeated balance of payments crises, accumulated arrears in foreign debt, slower economic growth, and declining per capita income (table 2.5). The momentum of development was halted and economic problems became increasingly pressing.

Foreign currency receipts declined sharply in Egypt, Syria, and Jordan beginning in 1982. Official transfers declined in Syria from an average of $1,620 million a year during the peak years of 1979-1981 to $770 million in 1987 and $530 million in 1988 (table 2.3). In Jordan, aid receipts declined from more than $1,200 million a year during the peak years to $600 million in 1987 and $566 million in 1988. Remittances from workers abroad to Egypt declined from a peak of $3.2 to $3.9 billion a year during 1983-1985 to $2.8 billion in 1987 (table 2.2). In Jordan gross remittances remained at $1.1 to 1.2 billion during the years 1982-1984, declining to $900 million in 1988.[14] Workers' remittances also declined in Syria, although figures are difficult to pin down because of missing entries in the balance of payments data and because of fluctuating exchange rates that affected their conversion.[15]

Rising balance of payments deficits and mounting external debt

To finance the enormous gap between imports and exports of non-oil goods (table 2.6), the three countries had become dependent on unstable external sources. The decline in foreign aid and other foreign currency earnings and the leveling off and decline in workers' remittances left the countries incapable of servicing their mounting foreign debts. International commercial banks and foreign suppliers reacted by refusing to extend further credit, which worsened the already shaky external balance. The current account deficit reached its peak in Egypt in 1985-1986 at 20 percent of GDP—14 percent if figures include official transfers. The current account deficit in Jordan peaked in 1983 at 31 percent of GDP—10 percent with official transfers. In Syria the deficit reached 11 percent of GDP in 1984—about 5 percent with transfers.[16]

These enormous non-oil trade deficits were financed mainly by the surplus in the services account (especially by workers' remittances), by official unilateral transfers, by foreign credit, and—in Egypt's case—by earnings from oil exports. This pattern of financing was especially true in Egypt and Syria because agricultural and industrial exports had not increased in current dollars in the first half of the 1980s and therefore had declined significantly in real terms (table 2.6). Exports had increased in Jordan—but almost totally in such export-oriented products as phosphates, potash, and chemical fertilizers.

The continuing large balance of payments deficits in Egypt led, by the end of 1987, to the accumulation of more than $40 billion in foreign debt—including $4.5 billion in short-term debt and $1.1 billion in private unguaranteed long-term debt. Indeed, foreign debt exceeded Egypt's GNP, an estimated $36 billion in 1987.[17] The structure of foreign debt deteriorated as the proportion of nonconcessionary loans increased. Egypt's foreign debt increased rapidly after 1982, as its balance of payments weakened. In the four years between June 1983 and June 1987, Egypt's foreign debt—excluding the medium- and long-term debt of the private sector—increased $10 billion, from $27.6 to $37.6 billion.[18]

Payment obligations on the principal and interest reached $4.8 billion in 1985-1986 (table 2.7)—roughly 48 percent of Egypt's earnings from the export of goods and services that year. The ratio of debt service to GNP reached 12.7 percent. Egypt could not keep up with such large payments and ceased to honor its foreign obligations. Arrears reached $3.1 billion by the end of 1986, to which another $500 million in interest was added in May 1987. At that time, representatives of 18 of Egypt's creditor states met under the auspices of the Paris Club and agreed to spread out principal, interest, and arrears due for payments over 10 years: a five-year grace period followed by 10 equal payments every six months. This agreement reduced Egypt's debt-service obligations from $4.8 billion in 1985-1986 to $2.5 billion in 1987 (table 2.7).

Despite the rescheduling agreements and a big drop in Egyptian imports —from a peak of $10.5 billion in 1985 to $7.8 billion in 1986-1987—the foreign debt problem will continue to plague the Egyptian economy for some time. Short-term emergency measures—such as tightening import controls or slowing down economic growth—are inappropriate remedies for a severe debt crisis. Instead, it is important to concentrate on developing export capabilities. Such a change of direction will be difficult as foreign suppliers and lenders to whom Egypt defaulted will be reluctant to renew or extend credit. The downward slide in Egypt's net capital account—from a positive $1,950 million in 1986[19] to a deficit of $950 million in 1987—no doubt reflects the reluctance of lenders to throw good money after bad. Egypt is now forced to finance not only the current deficit (almost $3 billion in 1987) but a net capital outflow of about $1 billion a year as well. Since the 1987 rescheduling agreement, new external arrears on previous years' loans continued to accumulate to an estimated $10.7 billion as of June 1989.[20]

New and more comprehensive data reveal a much more serious foreign debt problem for Jordan than earlier data had suggested. A rapid rise in indebtedness in the 1980s brought the total stock of Jordan's medium- and long-term government-guaranteed foreign debt at the end of 1989 to an unsustainable $8 billion, excluding military loans.[21] This sum amounts to 160 percent of Jordan's GNP. On top of that, short-term external debt is an estimated $400 million. The debt-servicing obligations have reached enormous dimensions: an estimated $860 million in 1988, and even more in 1989. This amount, which exceeds total merchandise exports, is obviously unsustainable. Jordan started negotiations with the IMF in March 1989 for a stabilization program. In addition, it has started negotiations through the Paris Club with official lenders, and through the London Club with private international banks, on rescheduling agreements for loans due in 1989 and 1990.

The situation in Syria is unclear because data published by Syrian authorities and international agencies do not include Syria's military debt to the Soviet Union, apparently sizable.[22] Other components of Syria's foreign debt also seem to be omitted from official data. According to World Bank figures (known to be underestimates), Syria's total external debt amounted to $4.7 billion—or 25 percent of GNP—at the end of 1987. With the balance of payments weakening, Syria had trouble repaying its debts to foreign countries. It was forced to reach rescheduling agreements with Iran in 1984 and with Czechoslovakia and the Soviet Union in 1986-1987.

THE UNDERLYING STRUCTURAL PROBLEMS

To correct the balance of payments and deal with foreign debt, Egypt, Syria, and Jordan had to take forceful steps. Recently their governments took steps to limit imports and implement a restrictive macroeconomic policy. Their efforts to reduce both budget and foreign trade deficits reflect their awareness of how the two deficits are connected. A policy of budgetary restraint, combined with a decline in workers' remittances, has reduced domestic consumption, investments, and imports in all three countries. Imports have declined significantly since 1982 in Jordan, since 1984 in Syria, and since 1985 in Egypt, also due to difficulties in obtaining import financing abroad.[23] Economic growth first slowed down and then declined (table 2.5), and both private consumption and investments contracted sharply (tables 1.3 to 1.5 and figures 1.1). Syria experienced an absolute decline in private consumption and its standard of living, because of decreases in workers' remittances and the erosion of real wages, as nominal wages lagged behind the rise in consumer prices. Consumer prices rose because the government abolished subsidies and took other policy steps that partly revived inflation in the short run. During 1982-1987, real per capita private consumption in Syria declined 34 percent—nearly reducing it to the standard of living before the boom (table 1.5).

Economic policies

Reducing imports, investments, and public and private domestic demand—crucial as those stabilization measures may be for preventing economic collapse—will not by themselves bring about economic recovery. The purpose of stabilization policy is to provide a transition period in which the effects of an economic crisis can be alleviated. Fundamental economic change—the need for which the crisis demonstrates—requires by its nature an extended period. Successful stabilization efforts and easier terms for repaying external debt are important to get the economy functioning normally in the short run, but they are no substitute for the structural change crucial to sustained economic growth. Without structural change, the three countries' balance of payments crises will become chronic.

What Egypt, Syria, and Jordan need for long-term growth is to reorient their economies to external markets, relying more on diversified exports. For these small economies to achieve sustained growth and a high standard of living, they must be integrated into the world market. Economic distortions now limit their economic efficiency, especially in Egypt and Syria. To protect domestic production, these governments have controlled imports and set high tariffs—policies that perpetuate the inefficiency and uncompetitiveness they were designed to reduce.

Developing an external orientation means opening the economy to foreign competition and integrating it more rapidly into the world economy. In both Egypt and Syria, merchandise exports (excluding petroleum) are low at only 4 percent of GNP. Syria's exports of goods, excluding petroleum, were only $650 million in 1987, Egypt's only $1,360 million. These volumes are low in comparison to other economies of similar size that have diversified their economies, become more efficient, and joined the world economy. Exports of goods from Jordan—a more open economy with fewer price distortions—amounted to $735 million in 1987. This is relatively greater than those from the other two nations, and even exceeds in absolute size those of Syria despite Syria's economy being four times bigger than Jordan's. But even in Jordan exports of goods have not exceeded 12 to 14 percent of GNP in recent years.[24] (The type of policy reform and structural adjustment needed to significantly increase non-oil exports in the three economies is discussed in chapter 7.)

Demographics

Two major problems make long-term growth difficult in the three economies: demographic developments and the arms race. Discussed more fully in chapters 4 and 6, they deserve brief comment here. Rapid population growth is not unique to the Middle East; indeed, it is common in developing countries. It does limit the growth capabilities of the three economies, however—especially that of Egypt, which is both poorer and more populous than Syria and Jordan. Between 1982 and 1987 the population growth rate in Egypt was 2.7 percent a year, and in Syria and Jordan it reached 3.7 percent,[25] rates among the highest in the world. Population explosions of this magnitude put a heavy burden on resources that are already in short supply. Proportionately more investments are needed to absorb the growing population, because of the need to extend public services, build housing, and create new jobs. What is left for increasing the per capita stock of capital—needed for increasing productivity and average incomes—is often reduced to half of the new fixed investments.

The demographic problem also affects the age structure of the three countries. The youngest age group (under 15 years of age) is proportionately very high—more than 45 percent of the general population, compared with 22 percent to 25 percent in industrial countries. These countries thus have a high "dependency" ratio made even higher because women participate so little in the active labor force.[26] Only 25 to 27 percent of the residents of Egypt, Syria, and Jordan are active in the labor force, compared with more than 45 percent in industrial countries. The fact that a relatively small number of producers supports a large number of consumers limits the average level of income and savings—and the economy's ability to invest and grow. Workers in these countries would have to be twice as productive as workers in industrial countries to achieve an equivalent per capita income. A growth-oriented economic program should therefore emphasize policies to reduce birth rates, particularly in Egypt.

Heavy military spending

Heavy defense spending also burdens many countries in the Middle East. Of the 14 nations with the highest ratio of defense expenditures to GNP in 1985—ratios above 10 percent—11 were Middle Eastern countries.[27] The ratio of military spending to GNP exceeded 25 percent in Syria and Israel in the early 1980s, reached 20 percent in Jordan in 1985-1986, and peaked at 18 percent in Egypt in 1972. The ratio in Egypt declined to between 10 and 12 percent in recent years, following the peace treaty with Israel. Military spending has been cut in Syria and Israel as well in recent years, because of stabilization efforts aimed at limiting economic deterioration. As a result, the ratio of military spending to GNP in 1986 declined to 23 percent in Syria and to 18 percent in Israel (table 6.6). In most developing countries this ratio ranges from 2 percent to 4 percent. Domestic military expenditures (excluding arms imports) as a proportion of GDP—the preferred indicator of economic defense burdens in the three Arab states and Israel—has in recent years been between 14 and 15 percent in Syria and Jordan, between 12 and 15 percent in Israel, and more than 8 percent in Egypt (tables 6.1 and 6.4). Such heavy spending on defense—even if financed with special foreign aid for arms imports—constitutes a heavy economic burden, diverting resources from productive uses and limiting long-term economic growth.

NOTES

1. World Bank 1989e.

2. Precise data on the extent of worker migration in the Middle East are not available. Estimates differ so greatly that they must be used with caution—merely to indicate trends and orders of magnitude.

3. Another quarter million foreign workers were in Libya, most of them Egyptian.

4. It is difficult to make even a rough estimate of the number of foreign workers in Iraq, because there are no official statistics on the subject.

5. The number of Jordanian workers abroad is estimated at 330,000. This apparently includes Palestinian workers from the West Bank. About 85 percent of these Jordanian workers are employed in the oil-producing Arab countries of the Persian Gulf—over half of them in Saudi Arabia. The domestic Jordanian labor force was estimated to be 535,000 in 1986. In addition, Jordan imports about 130,000 workers, mainly from Egypt, to work in agriculture, construction, and other services for which there are labor shortages. Foreign workers, most of whom are nonprofessional, constituted about 20 percent of Jordan's domestic labor force in 1986.

6. In 1979, official unilateral transfers surged to $1.6 billion for Syria and more than $1 billion for Jordan.

7. Excluding workers' remittances.

8. In 1987, the export of crude oil and oil products reached $700 million—offset by $400 million in imports of oil products. In 1988, exports were $585 million, imports $200 million.

9. The economic situation in Iran began to deteriorate in 1978, with the Islamic revolution. Economic conditions began to deteriorate in Iraq in 1980, with the outbreak of the Iraq-Iran War.

10. Total aid from OAPEC (Organization of Arab Petroleum Exporting Countries) in 1981 was $8.2 billion. Saudi Arabia's share was 67 percent. Saudi Arabia employed about half of all foreign workers in the Gulf states.

11. Total foreign aid from the OAPEC countries decreased from a peak of $9.5 billion in 1980 to $3.3 billion in 1987. World Bank 1989d.

12. Payments from oil carriers constitute a large part of Suez Canal dues.

13. Including grants from abroad reduces the budget deficit figure. In 1982, for example, Syria's deficit, excluding grants, was 17.5 percent of GNP; allowing for grants, it was only 9.5 percent. Without grants, Jordan's deficit was 23.7 percent; grants reduced it to 8.5 percent. In 1982 Egypt's overall budget deficit was 19.1 percent of GDP.

14. The outflow of remittances from foreign workers in Jordan declined from $254 million in 1984 to $247 million in 1986 and $154 million in 1988.

15. Moreover, many of the transfers do not appear in the official statistics because they were exchanged on the free market.

16. Current deficits are underestimated for the three states because data on imports of military arms are not included in official balance of payments statistics. This subject is discussed in Chapter 6.

17. World Bank 1988b.

18. IMF data. In 1974 Egypt's public and publicly guaranteed long-term external debt (the bulk of total debt) was less than $3 billion. During the period of prosperity—between 1975 and 1981—it increased $16 billion, reaching $19 billion at the end of 1981 (World Bank 1989e).

19. Including net investments of $200 million a year.

20. IMF data. This figure includes obligations to certain Arab creditor countries and to the Gulf Organization for Development of Egypt (GODE), with which there seems to be a tacit agreement not to reschedule or to service their claims.

21. IMF data and statements in the media by Jordan's Finance Minister and the Governor of Jordan's Central Bank.

22. Unofficial sources in the Financial Times of September 1989 estimate Syria's external military debt at $15 billion.

23. Increases in merchandise imports were registered in Egypt in 1988 and in 1989 (table 2.6), largely because of higher food import prices.

24. Figures here are based on IMF data. It is worth noting that exports account for 45 percent of industrial production in Israel and 30 percent of agricultural production. In Taiwan—a country with a population of 20 million in 1988 and a GNP of $100 billion—merchandise exports amounted to $60 billion.

25. See table 2.5. Egypt's population growth rate would double the population in 25 years; Syria's and Jordan's would double theirs in only 18 years.

26. In 1987, females represented only 16.5 percent of the labor force in Syria, and only 9.6 percent of the labor force in Jordan and Egypt. (World Bank 1989e.)

27. The other three countries were North Korea, Nicaragua, and the Soviet Union. (ACDA 1988, p. 32.)

Table 2.1 Annual Real Rates of Growth, 1973-1987
(percentages)

	GDP (at factor cost)		GDP (at factor cost) per capita	
	1973-1981	*1982-1987*	*1973-1981*	*1982-1987*
Egypt	8.9	6.2[b]	*6.0*	*3.4*
Syria[a]	8.6	-1.1	*4.9*	*-4.6*
Jordan	10.6	3.8	*8.0*	*0.1*

a. GDP at market prices.
b. Recent preliminary figures for 1987-1989 indicate stagnation in GDP.
Source: World Bank 1989e.

Table 2.2 Receipts of Workers' Remittances
(in $US millions)

	Egypt	Syria[a]	Jordan[b]
1970	29	7	16
1972	104	40	21
1974	189	45	75
1980	2,696	774	640
1981	2,855	581	875
1982	1,935	446	907
1983	3,166	461	909
1984	3,930	327	983
1985	3,500	293	787
1986	2,973	251	938
1987	2,845	250	754
1988	3,400*	210*	749*

a. Published data in Syria refer to private transfers, but most of this is believed to be workers' remittances. Official accounts of such transfers are probably underestimated, since an increasing part of it has been converted on the free market to take advantage of higher exchange rates, particularly in recent years. In 1979, recorded private transfers exceeded $900 million.

b. Net remittances, after subtracting remittances for foreign workers in Jordan, which amounted to $254 million in 1984, $231 million in 1986, $184 million in 1987, and $154 million in 1988.

* Preliminary figures.
Source: World Bank 1989e, IMF data.

Table 2.3 Official Transfers to the Public Sector
(in $US millions)

	Egypt[a]	Syria	Jordan
1972[b]	(300)	(45)	(190)
1974[b]	1,260	(410)	(260)
1978	382	782	348
1979	291	1,627	1,046
1980	72	1,510	1,335
1981	279	1,711	1,258
1982	791	1,398	1,032
1983	772	1,304	798
1984	1,097	1,230	681
1985	1,209	1,090	739
1986	974	760	633
1987	700*	770	600
1988	800*	530	566

a. Data for Egypt, from 1980 on, refer to years starting in July and ending in June of the next calendar year.
b. Figures in parentheses may include private transfers.
* Preliminary figures.
Source: World Bank 1989e, and IMF data.

Table 2.4 Foreign Currency Receipts, 1972, 1982, 1987
($US millions)

	Egypt			Syria			Jordan		
	1972	1982	1987	1972	1982	1987	1972	1982	1987
Workers' remittances (net)	100	3,170	2,840	40	450*	250*	20	910	730
Official transfers	300	790	970	451	1,400	770	190	1,030	600
Oil exports (net)	—	2,470	1,220	—	—	210	—	—	—
Suez Canal dues	—	960	1,150	—	—	—	—	—	—
Total four items	400	7,390	6,180	85	1,850	1,230	210	1,940	1,330
Non-oil merchandise exports	820	1,090	1,360	235	480	650	48	530	720

* Underreported in 1982 and 1987. See footnote b to table 2.2.
Source: World Bank 1989e and various issues and IMF, *International Financial Statistics*, various issues.

Table 2.5 Annual Real Rates of Growth, 1982-1987
(percentage)

	1982	1983	1984	1985	1986	1987	Average 1982-1987
Total GDP **(at factor cost)**							
Egypt	11.5	7.6	6.2	6.7	2.7	2.5	6.2[b]
Syria	3.0	1.8	-3.6	3.0	-1.2	-9.5	-1.1
Jordan	8.9	2.2	8.2	1.6	3.7	-1.5	3.8
Population							
Egypt	2.9	2.8	2.7	2.6	2.5	2.4	2.7
Syria	3.5	3.5	3.6	3.6	3.7	3.7	3.6
Jordan	3.5	3.7	3.7	3.7	3.4	3.9	3.7
Per capita GDP							
Egypt	8.4	4.7	3.4	4.0	0.2	0.1	3.4
Syria[a]	-0.5	-1.6	-6.9	-0.6	-4.7	-12.4	-4.6
Jordan	5.2	-1.4	4.3	-2.6	0.3	-5.2	0.1

a. GDP at market prices.
b. See footnote (b) in table 2.1.
Source: World Bank 1989e.

Table 2.6 Nonfuel Merchandise Imports and Exports, 1972-1987
($US millions, current prices)

	Egypt		Syria		Jordan[a]	
	Imports	*Exports*	*Imports*	*Exports*	*Imports*	*Exports*
1972	840	820	515	235	254	48
1980	9,063	1,128	2,973	443	2,020	403
1981	8,978	1,112	2,995	415	2,640	509
1982	9,040	1,087	2,135	480	2,584	527
1983	10,287	1,393	2,660	585	2,450	441
1984	10,516	1,294	2,285	658	2,230	680
1985	9,527	1,198	2,390	447	2,155	648
1986	7,760	1,361	1,870	476	2,090	645
1987	9,800*	1,700*	1,740	650	2,230	735
1988	10,100*	1,500*	1,640	680	2,320	874

a. Excluding transit exports to Iraq.
* Preliminary figures.
Source: IMF data, World Bank 1989e.

Table 2.7 Egypt's External Debt Service Obligations, 1982-1983 to 1986-1987
($US billions)

	1982-1983	1983-1984	1984-1985	1985-1986	1986-1987*
Amortization[a]	1.6	2.0	1.8	2.6	1.3
Interest	1.6	1.9	2.3	2.2	1.2
Total debt service	3.2	3.9	4.1	4.8	2.5
Current account receipts[b]	10.7	11.9	11.4	9.9	9.6
In percentage of current receipts	30.1	33.2	36.6	48.2	26.2

a. Medium and long-term public and publicly guaranteed debt only.
b. Excluding official grants.
* Preliminary, after rescheduling.
Source: IMF data.

3

THE INADEQUACY OF DOMESTIC POLICY

A big drop in foreign resources for current and development budgets precipitated the current economic crisis in Egypt, Syria, and Jordan. Worsening that external shock, however, were heavy defense spending, a bias growth in nontradables during the period of prosperity, and the governments' later failure to adjust properly to declining oil prices, external aid, and remittances from workers abroad. Although external shocks and government policies both contributed to the inefficient use of resources, the focus of reform should be on policy change. Unless government policies are corrected, any foreign exchange that comes in may bring temporary relief but no lasting benefits. In this chapter we discuss how domestic policies—or policy inadequacies—caused and then aggravated the crisis of the 1980s.

UNBALANCED GROWTH AND THE BIAS TOWARD NONTRADABLES

In recent decades, development has brought about remarkable structural changes in the economies of Egypt, Syria, Jordan, and many other developing countries. As a result of changing patterns of demand and development, agriculture's role in the economy has declined, and services and industry have become more important. The large, poor, traditional agricultural sector was clearly a barrier to economic growth in the Middle East. Before World War II roughly two-thirds of the people in Egypt, Syria, and Jordan worked in agriculture, producing nearly half the GDP. The poor and poorly educated rural population made little use of advanced technology. Agricultural production was labor-intensive, and per capita agricultural production was low. The export of a small surplus of agricultural produce and meager imports of industrial products satisfied the limited demand of the poor population. A few modern industrial plants produced food, textiles, and building materials for the local market, but most of the industrial sector was still at the handicraft stage. Less than 8 percent of the working population was employed in industry—mostly in small workshops.

World War II brought dramatic political changes—independence and coups d'etat—to many Middle Eastern states, changing their economies. The new regimes emphasized education, modernization, and economic development. Foreign economic aid and technical assistance from the industrial countries provided the impetus for change and faster economic development. Egypt and Syria became centrally planned economies, whose governments took on the role of stimulating economic development (Lavy 1990). Their large private enterprises were nationalized, the central government made most of the investments in the economy, and the public sector became increasingly large. In time, the public sector's inefficiency would aggravate economic problems and limit sustained economic growth. In Jordan, by contrast, the government took a more limited role in the economy, and despite total or partial public ownership of several large economic enterprises, the system was more open to private initiative.

Postwar political changes and economic growth in the 1950s and 1960s brought significant socioeconomic changes to Egypt, Syria, and Jordan (Lavy 1987). The most significant change was a shift in emphasis from the agricultural sector to industry and services. The rapid growth of those urban sectors was reflected in a population shift from rural to urban areas, which changed the structure of the economy and society. Industrialization and urbanization in a backward economy do not simply increase output. They bring about upheavals in the values, outlook, and way of life of traditional agrarian society. Today half the people of Egypt and Syria and 70 percent of those in Jordan live in urban areas, mostly large cities. Even in the villages more and more people work not in agriculture but in services, construction, handicrafts, and industry.

The changes that started after World War II continued at a faster pace between 1973 and 1982, the decade of prosperity. But the special circumstances that brought an influx of foreign currency to the three economies influenced that accelerated growth. The increase in foreign currency receipts, not based on increased exports, permitted more imports of goods and made it possible for the economy to specialize in nontradables. Services and construction, for example, grew at an unprecedented rate, and their share in GDP and employment rose dramatically at the same time that agriculture's share fell. Manufacturing maintained more or less the same share as before, because more manufactured goods were imported to satisfy the needs of the rapidly expanding local market.

What do such heavy influxes of foreign currency imply? Work on the "Dutch disease"[1] suggests a possible causal link between a heavy influx of foreign currency and an unbalanced pattern of growth. In this context, the effects of foreign aid, oil revenues, and workers' remittances are similar, since earning them does not require allocating means of production domestically or expanding the export sector. They can all be treated as windfall income.

The transfer of foreign exchange mainly as foreign aid or oil export windfalls—because partly spent on nontraded goods—puts upward pressure on the real exchange rate (the price of nontraded goods relative to traded goods). When domestic income increases, an increase in this ratio shifts production to nontradables and demand to tradables. Real income increases, through more absorption of nontradables and more net imports of tradables. How does this affect the allocation of resources? Labor shifts out of agriculture into services (often urban), real wages go up (in terms of export goods), and the country becomes less competitive in international markets. A decline in export performance is then unavoidable unless specific policy measures are taken to counteract it.

Traditionally, the only way to finance an increase in industrial imports (whether for consumption or investment) was to increase agricultural and other exports. As the economy grows, more imports are needed—but to be able to increase imports the country has to increase exports, to earn foreign exchange. Foreign loans to finance imports are seen only as a temporary measure: increasing foreign debt beyond a certain level was unsustainable, since it implied high annual repayments in foreign currency, which was scarce.

This was the approach Egypt, Syria, Jordan, and other developing countries had taken until 1973. After 1973, however, foreign currency flowed into the three economies as a result of the oil boom, so financing was available to increase imports without expanding agricultural and industrial exports. In Egypt, for example, the receipts from four "special" items—foreign aid, oil exports, workers' remittances, and Suez Canal dues—increased from $400 million in 1972 to $7,400 million in 1982.[2] In Syria the receipts from "special" items increased from $80 million to $1,800 million, and in Jordan from $200 million to almost $2,000 million (table 2.4).

Moreover, traditional agricultural and industrial exports actually decreased in real terms during the boom in Egypt and Syria because of increased local demand and overvalued exchange rates. Both countries began to show a deficit in the foreign trade account in agricultural produce.[3] Only Jordan increased its industrial exports—because of exportable natural resources and the maturing of its investments in the first half of the 1980s in phosphate extraction and the production of potash and chemical fertilizers. But even in Jordan, exports of other industrial products did not increase significantly.

The process of urbanization and the decline in agriculture was intensified in Egypt, Syria, and Jordan during the boom. Agricultural employment did not grow significantly in the 1970s and 1980s, despite a rapid increase in the civilian labor force. And as a share of total employment, it declined—in Egypt, from 49 percent in 1974 to 37 percent in 1986, and in Syria from 43 percent to 30 percent. A jump in consumption of food and other agricultural produce was supplied largely by imports, as agricultural output grew only 2 to 3 percent a year. As a share of GDP, agriculture in Egypt declined from 30 percent in the early 1970s to about 17 percent in 1986-1987 and in Syria from 28 percent in the late 1960s to an annual average of about 21 percent between 1982 and 1986.[4]

Industry (excluding mining, water, and electricity) did not change much after the early 1970s. In 1987 it represented about 12 to 13 percent of GDP in Jordan and Syria and about 14 percent in Egypt, similar to the share in 1972. From 1973 on, industrialization mainly satisfied increased domestic demand. The rate of employment in industry also remained fairly constant. Any new manpower was absorbed in construction and the local service sectors (especially public services) or migrated to the oil-producing countries of the Persian Gulf after 1973.

The abundance of foreign currency allowed Egypt and Syria to maintain an overvalued exchange rate for many years. That, together with expanding domestic demand, encouraged the bias toward nontradables. Egypt and Syria concentrated on expanding services and producing goods for the domestic market, while imports expanded rapidly. Limited efforts were made to expand and develop a competitive export potential in industry, agriculture, and tourism, which could have provided foreign currency to repay foreign debt when the boom ended. In Jordan, where foreign aid and workers' remittances at one point reached 40 percent of GDP,[5] services represented an astonishing 64 percent of GDP in 1987, nearly a world record. In both Syria and Egypt services reached 54 percent of GDP in 1987. Compared with other developing countries at their income levels, all three countries had an overdeveloped service sector.[6]

As a share of GDP, construction also soared in the three countries—especially in Jordan, where it reached more than 9 percent of GDP in 1982 before declining to 6 percent in 1987, as the economy deteriorated and efforts were made to stabilize the economy. In Syria construction remained roughly 6 to 7 percent of GDP in 1982-1986, declining to 5.4 percent in 1987 and 4.8 percent in 1988. In Egypt construction reached 5.2 percent of GDP in 1982, then declined to 4.4 percent in 1987.

The bias toward nontradables was reflected most dramatically in heavy defense spending, especially in Syria and Jordan, and in expansion of the public sector. In Egypt and Syria, foreign currency receipts from official transfers (and in Egypt from oil exports and Suez Canal dues) went directly to the state treasury and stimulated government spending.

Egypt's experience is typical. Between 1974 and 1982, most new workers were absorbed by the nontradable sector. Nearly 68 percent of new workers were in services—half of them in the government, which sent the budget sky-high. The jump in service employees—nearly two-thirds of new workers, or about 2.5 million people—was dramatic (table 3.1). Within a short period, there were more employees in services (5 million in 1982) than in agriculture (4.3 million). Construction was the second most important employer of new workers. Only about 15 percent of Egypt's new workers went into agriculture and industry.[7]

After 1982, when foreign currency receipts declined, the pattern of unbalanced growth and the bias toward nontradables continued, financed mainly by short-term foreign credit. Adjustments to compensate for deteriorating external circumstances were delayed because new foreign credits continued to be available, although at a higher interest rate.

Multiple exchange rate systems continued in Egypt and Syria, so large fiscal deficits and extensive implicit subsidies persisted in all three countries. Not until 1987-1988—when the foreign debt crisis was severe and it was impossible to ignore the deterioration in balance of payments and internal stability—were serious steps taken to contain demand and to correct price distortions and the overvalued exchange rate. In Jordan the overvalued dinar was significantly depreciated from October 1988 through early 1989. Adjustments in Syrian exchange rates took effect in January 1988. In May 1987 Egypt established a new, flexible bank foreign exchange market which it hoped would replace the free nonbank market.

Devaluation—combined with partial unification of multiple exchange rates in Syria and Egypt—was important for the tradable sectors. But much more than that was needed to transform these economies structurally and to achieve sustained, export-led growth. For such sustained growth, all three countries needed to reduce public spending, restore sustained fiscal balance, remove price distortions, and establish more realistic unified exchange rates.

TRIMMING THE FAT IN THE PUBLIC SECTOR

Many of the economic difficulties the three countries face can be attributed to the rapid growth and inefficient management of their public sectors and to overambitious public investment programs. Wide-ranging public sector activities and the operating subsidies to public enterprises have stifled private enterpreneurial activity in agriculture, industry, and commerce. In the face of financial difficulties, all three countries have tried to reduce the size and improve the management of their public sectors. These reforms are still at an early stage, however.

The state plays a larger role in the economies of the Middle East than in other regions. More than 40 percent of the civilian labor force in Egypt—and more than half that in Syria and Jordan—is employed by the public sector, compared with only one third of the civilian labor force in Asia. In Egypt government spending came to 45 percent, and government revenues to only 28 percent, of estimated GDP, in 1987.

The three countries have more public enterprises engaged in more types of activities than most other developing countries. Egypt especially has a large public enterprise sector—and provides substantial explicit and implicit subsidies through a highly overvalued exchange rate for commodity imports and by financing public enterprise losses with external loans and accumulated debts. In Syria all utilities, all banking and financial enterprises, and all large-scale mining, manufacturing, and construction enterprises, are publicly owned. Public enterprises also play an important role in domestic and foreign trade. In Jordan the role of the government in the economy is somewhat less dominant. Most nonfinancial public enterprises are autonomous, although some of them depend financially on the central government. The central government also participates, through joint ownership, in many enterprises and is represented on their boards.

To make matters worse, other sources of revenue, including direct and indirect taxes, fell. In Egypt revenues as a percentage of GDP fell from 45 percent in 1980-1981 to 35 percent in 1984-1985—mostly because of falling oil prices and a decline in surpluses of public enterprises. Customs duties, Egypt's second most important source of revenues, declined as imports fell. Personal income tax, which brought in less than half a percent of GDP (collected mainly from public employees), showed limited elasticity and remained a marginal source of revenue.

In Egypt during the first half of the 1980s, total spending (in current prices) rose about 13 percent a year, current spending 14 percent a year, and capital spending almost 12 percent a year. The increase in current spending was due largely to expanded resources for public service authorities (interest payments on government debt and subsidies) and somewhat less to general public services (public enterprise losses) and defense. The overall deficit grew 20 percent a year, but a smaller proportion of it was externally financed. The deficit and the resulting excess demand pressures led to a severe balance of payments problem. By 1986 arrears on external debt service had reached US $3.2 billion, and external debt-service obligations were equivalent to nearly half of current receipts. Government reliance on domestic loans to finance the fiscal deficit sharply increased total credit and net domestic assets. This credit expansion intensified inflationary and balance of payments pressures. The deficit was financed mainly by rescheduling an estimated US $3.1 billion in external debt and the accrual of just over half a billion in new arrears.

THE FISCAL DEFICIT AND FOREIGN FINANCE

As a share of GDP, government spending for 1981-1985 averaged 60 percent in Egypt, 44 percent in Syria, and 48 percent in Jordan (excluding arms imports).[8] With government spending so heavy and revenues lagging, fiscal deficits represented a large proportion of GDP: 23 and 22 percent in Egypt in 1983 and 1984 respectively, 21 percent in Syria in 1984, and 31 percent in Jordan in 1980 (table 3.2). These huge fiscal deficits (table 3.3) were the result of expanding goverment services and social expenditures (in Egypt), large military and defense budgets (in Syria and Jordan), and ambitious investment programs (in Jordan). Earlier, the governments had relied heavily on foreign aid and external loans to finance the deficits. Foreign aid for Egypt had come mainly from the United States, for Syria from the Arab countries, and for Jordan from Arabs and the West. The aid not only helped finance the budget gap but, more important, had paid for the heavy imports that bridged the gap between heavy domestic demand and light domestic output. The budget deficit was thus translated into a balance of payments deficit with little effect on prices.

When the oil slump came in 1982, these external sources of foreign exchange declined. Imports were drastically curtailed, and the three countries had to borrow from domestic and international banks to finance the deficit. As a share of GDP, external financing of the budget deficit dropped in Egypt from 5 percent in 1979 to 3.5 percent in 1983-1984, in Syria from 18 percent in 1979 to 3.0 percent in 1986-1987, and in Jordan from 31 percent in 1979 to 8 percent in 1987. This structural change in deficit financing led to higher inflation,[9] shortages of raw material imports, and a record external debt.

Fiscal performance in Syria also declined significantly in 1982-1985, because of a decline in the growth of fiscal revenues, the deteriorating financial position of public enterprises, and a drop in external grants (table 3.3). Outlays for defense and subsidies accounted for more than half the increase for 1982-1986. The second highest expense, after defense, is the transfer to public enterprises for subsidies and replenishments of working capital.[10] With the decline of external grants, most of Syria's fiscal deficit was financed by domestic borrowing. Domestic borrowing climbed from an average LS 5.5 billion in 1982-1983 to LS 9.8 billion in 1984-1985, nearly 17 percent of the stock of money and quasimoney in 1982-1983. Net domestic assets rose about 25 percent a year, mainly from a 43 percent net increase in credit to the government. Because the government deficit was so large, the external deficit almost tripled —from US $270 million in 1982 to more than US $770 million in 1985. The cumulative deficit for this four-year period was about US $2.3 billion.[11] One result of intensified demand pressure was rapid inflation; the wholesale price index rose 44 percent in 1986.[12]

Revenues in Syria remained stable as a share of GDP in the 1980s because a sharp increase in tax revenues offset a decline in nontax revenues. Nontax revenues fell largely because of a 32-percent decline in receipts from public enterprises in manufacturing, mining, and construction between 1983 and 1986—reflecting in particular the reduced operating surplus of the Syrian Petroleum Company. During the same period, revenues from income and profit taxes rose because of improved procedures in tax collection.

As external grants continued to decline, Syria began in 1985 to make serious efforts to reduce the fiscal deficit and contain aggregate demand. Syria cut its deficit to 5.7 percent of GDP in 1987, about a quarter of its early 1980s' level. It did so mainly through tight controls on government hiring, investment, and purchases. Revenues remained about 25 percent of GDP, but total spending declined from 47 percent of GDP in 1984 to 30 percent in 1987, more than compensating for the decline in external grants.

Jordan made no appropriate adjustments to the region's economic slowdown, declining transfers, and limited export growth. To maintain the momentum of economic activity in the early 1980s, the government kept public sector spending high. As a result the budget deficit rose from 15 percent of GDP in 1984 to 24 percent in 1988, which included an increase in grants from 8.5 percent of GDP to more than 16 percent. Jordan financed its deficit by external borrowing contracted on increasingly nonconcessional terms until 1987, when domestic borrowing increased.

PUBLIC ENTERPRISES OUT OF CONTROL: A LOOK AT EGYPT

Egypt's public enterprises illustrate the effect on the current crisis in all three countries. Until the early 1950s the Egyptian economy was essentially oriented to the private sector. But beginning in 1956, Egypt witnessed the emergence of a public sector that, through a series of nationalization decrees, gradually assumed control over many production activities. By 1973 public enterprises accounted for 47 percent of value added and 28 percent of employment. Agriculture was the only activity for which the public sector did not assume direct control of production.

Only in 1973, as economic difficulties mounted, did President Sadat announce a shift in Egypt's development strategy toward an open-door policy. The focus of the new policy was a shift from the inward-looking development strategy Egypt had followed since 1952 toward a more outward-oriented strategy, geared to taking advantage of international finance, technology, and markets. The strategy was not a radical break with the past, however. The private sector's share in value added and investment did go up (from 22 percent in the early 1970s to 33 percent in 1987),[13] but the public sector continued to dominate all production activities except agriculture. As many as 372 public companies were supervised by 18 ministries.

Under the present economic structure, the performance of public enterprises has a decisive influence on Egypt's development prospects. The economy's ability to sustain a high rate of growth in output, investment, and consumption is greatly influenced by public enterprise output and savings. And the high cost of the public sector is a key factor in Egypt's deteriorating economic situation.

State-owned enterprises absorb almost 45 percent of total fixed investment, account for 40 percent of GDP, and generate about 83 percent of exports of goods and nonfactor services. Financially, the sector has a large and growing deficit, a low savings rate, a low and weakening rate of return, and a big chunk of Egypt's mounting external debt. The sector's deficit, expressed as a share of GDP, has remained high (at almost 10 percent) since 1982.[14] Public companies have contributed much more to the deficit than public authorities have. The net transfers from the treasury to public enterprises has been substantial (table 3.4).

The deficit, low savings rate, and heavy fiscal burden are all the result of structural inefficiencies and the low rate of return on public enterprise capital. For example the average gross rate of return on assets of public companies for 1980-1984 was only 8.25 percent.[15] For example the average net rate of return was only 5.5 percent, having fallen from 9 percent in 1973. The aggregate rate of return for public authorities (excluding the income from petroleum and the Suez Canal) was negative. The enterprises that showed the most negative rates of return were the Egyptian Railways, the Cairo and Alexandria transport authorities, and the Cairo and Alexandria Water and Sewage authorities. The Electricity Authority had a positive rate of return, but it was less than 3 percent in 1985.

As the financial difficulties of these enterprises mounted, the government resorted to long-term borrowing. What increased debt the most, however, were short-term loans and arrears. As deficits grew in public companies, the government allowed them to borrow heavily from public commercial banks. Public enterprises are not allowed to borrow from the private sector, so domestic financing for them had to come from the national budget or the public banking sector—increasing domestic credit, national fiscal deficits, and balance of payments deficits.

By mid-1985 the publicly guaranteed medium- and long-term civilian debt was reported at US $17 billion.[16] Other external banking system obligations were an estimated US $10.6 billion, of which US $5.6 billion was short-term debt. Public enterprises owed more than a third of the civilian medium- and long-term debt. Assuming that the distribution of the US $10.6 billion debt is about the same—a third owed by public enterprises—public enterprises accounted for about US $10 billion in foreign debt. This estimate may be conservative since public enterprises are believed to be responsible for about US $5 billion in unclassified long-term debt. Debt-service payments scheduled for 1985 were US $3.9 billion, public enterprises service obligation was about US $1.4 billion.

The problem is, public enterprises cannot service their debt. Public enterprise exports of goods and services grew only 16 percent in nominal dollar terms between 1974 and 1985, and much of that growth was from oil and Suez Canal revenues (table 3.5). Since 1979, oil and Suez Canal revenues accounted for more than 55 percent of exported goods and services—and more than 70 percent of public enterprise exports. Other public sector exports grew less than 3 percent a year in nominal dollar terms. And the corresponding export price index increased only 6 percent a year, so real exports declined more than 3 percent a year. What is worse, more than 90 percent of public enterprise debt is from enterprises unrelated to petroleum or the Suez Canal. Of the estimated US $1.4 billion debt service obligation attributable to public enterprises, nearly US $1.2 billion is the obligation of these "other" enterprises.

DISTORTED ECONOMIC POLICIES: EGYPT AND SYRIA

As a result of continuous government intervention and distortionary economic policies, Egypt and Syria have developed inefficient and uncompetitive economic systems incapable of supporting self-sustained long-term growth. These systems feature multiple exchange rates, administered prices, and heavy subsidies of many consumer goods and services—distorting production and reducing economic efficiency. Most of the analysis in this section focuses on Egypt and Syria. We refer only occasionally to Jordan, whose economy is relatively open and competitive, with limited government intervention and with prices and resource allocation determined largely by market forces.

Price controls and subsidies

Most prices in Egypt and Syria are determined administratively, with no regard for cost. Prices for many products provided by public authorities and enterprises are significantly lower than their cost of production or their prices on the world market. This is especially true of prices for energy, public transport, and basic food products. One objective of such policies is to provide at low cost to low-income groups such basic products as bread, electricity, gas, and public transportation. The idea is to increase the real income of the poor, who spend a large share of their income on these products. Some of the subsidized goods are rationed, so a black market flourishes. Agricultural prices are controlled to provide lower priced inputs for the food and textile industry and to keep inflation down.

This pricing policy wastes resources, distorts the allocation of resources, reduces efficiency in production and consumption, increases the fiscal deficit, and ultimately lowers the national savings rate. The increased fiscal deficit causes larger balance of payments deficits, causes higher inflation (to the extent that part of the deficit is financed by printing new money). The subsidies for two main exports—energy and cotton—increase their domestic consumption and therefore reduce exports.

Egypt. The importance of the subsidy system in Egypt is understated because most nontax incentives are seldom explicitly identified as subsidies in the national budget and others are provided for outside the budget accounts. The subsidies for public housing and the Egyptian railway, for example, are part of the budget but are not separately identified. The most obvious example of an explicit subsidy outside the budget is the operating losses of the General Authority for Supply Commodities, which are only partly covered by budget provisions. The budget transfers of this authority represent only part of the cost of providing subsidized food. A more complete measure of the cost of food subsidies must take into account the authority's borrowing from the banking system.[17] Those figures represent more than two-fifths of total annual tax collection in Egypt, and an average 9 to 10 percent of GDP.

Implicit subsidies are also provided through the pricing and exchange rate system. The cost, for example, of five important commodities (wheat, wheat flour, edible oil, sugar, and tea) is underrated because they are imported at the overvalued central bank exchange rate, which understates the cost of foreign exchange as measured on the free market. The implicit cost of this practice varies according to the exchange rate, but it often exceeds LE 1 billion a year (some 3 percent of GDP).

In agriculture, farmers benefited from implicit and explicit subsidies on seeds, fertilizer, and pesticides. In turn they provided a sizable implicit subsidy by receiving low producer prices for cotton and wheat (Lavy 1983). Low producer prices for cotton augmented the modest explicit subsidy to the textile industry provided in the budget and allowed the industry to supply cloth cheaply to domestic consumers (thus reducing exports).

The low price paid to wheat producers caused a decline in domestic output in the 1980s. The low consumer price of wheat, on the other hand, caused consumption to increase about 5 percent a year—so wheat imports increased dramatically. The subsidy for bread and other wheat products amounted to $1.2 billion in 1983 (3 percent of GDP).[18] Cotton farmers responded to low producer prices by decreasing production, so this staple agricultural export declined in the 1980s. Egypt moved from a positive balance in agricultural trade in the early 1970s to a $2.6 billion deficit in 1985. Further, crops on which prices adjusted to the costs of production or that were not implicitly taxed—rice, onions, and beans, for example—replaced cotton and wheat in the crop rotation system. And the output of fruits, vegetables, and livestock—not covered by the price control system—grew the fastest of all agricultural products.

Moreover, other commodities that the General Authority for Supply Commodities supplies to consumers are imported at the premium commercial bank exchange rate, which increases the implicit subsidy LE 1 billion a year. The petroleum products marketed by this authority—at prices an average 30 percent below southern European ex-refinery prices—also represent an implicit subsidy of LE 2 billion (6 percent of GDP).[19]   Because of this subsidy, energy consumption grew 10 percent a year in the decade 1974-1984. The real price of energy products in Egypt declined a third between 1972 and 1984, and the price of electricity fell 60 percent in real terms, despite a trend in the rest of the world toward higher energy prices and reduced consumption. The price control system also provides implicit subsidies on many basic food items, energy, public utilities, and the output of the public industrial sector. Only small price increases were allowed for these products until 1986. In addition, direct controls were imposed on the prices of certain goods and services produced and sold by the private sector. In Egypt, for example, housing is subject to rent control and landlords have been permitted to increase rents only 1 percent a year since 1967.

Only in 1985, in a major shift of policy, has the Ministry of Supply liberalized pricing policies by allowing importers to use the free market rate of exchange to establish retail prices for food products the private sector is allowed to import. As a result, the price of food products has since increased 26 percent a year. After the latest reforms, the subsidy bill was 5.3 percent of GDP in fiscal 1988.

Syria.   Syria also has a comprehensive system of price controls, covering all major consumer goods, public and private sector imports, and goods produced by public and private enterprises. Basic food products (bread, flour, rice, sugar, tea, and vegetable oil) are sold only by public agencies and their prices are determined by the Ministerial Economic Committee. Most agricultural producer prices are established by the High Council of Agriculture. All housing units except recently built or luxury units are rent controlled.

The annual reported cost of the controlled price and subsidy system, including production subsidies to public enterprises, was LS 4.5 billion in 1981, roughly 7 percent of GDP. But not all subsidies appear in the budget. A substantial portion is borne by the Stabilization Fund, which subsidizes prices of essential consumer goods, covering the subsidy with surcharges on other goods. The subsidization of petroleum products is only partially recorded in expenditures, the rest being offset by the transfer of surpluses from the Syrian Petroleum Company. And part of the operating losses of public sector enterprises, financed by the Commercial Bank of Syria, are occasionally assumed by the government.

The control of producer crop prices, at levels well below international prices, has substantially distorted Syrian agriculture. For example, the domestic procurement price for all major internationally traded crops except cotton—particularly maize and sugar beets—has in recent years been high relative to international prices. And in view of declining world prices on some products (for example, wheat, maize, and sugar beets), the procurement prices are extremely high. Such high procurement prices distort resource allocation by encouraging high-cost marginal producers, giving relatively efficient producers excessive rents and diverting resources from production of other profitable but unsupported crops. Maintaining high output prices for major export crops and low consumer prices for basic foodstuff means huge subsidies for food processing and distribution, particularly in wheat production and processing. When farmers were being paid an average LS 1,230 a ton for soft wheat, and the government was importing flour for about LS 1,070 a ton, flour was being sold at LS 142.5 a ton to state bakeries to prepare a popularly priced bread (which cost roughly 13 percent of what the imported flour cost). For sugar, the retail price for the monthly 1.5 kilos per sugar ration is less than one-third the raw material cost of sugar beets. The unrationed price is barely equal to the raw material costs.

Subsidies of energy pricing are also common. Electricity tariff levels, for example, have fallen considerably in real terms (more than 40 percent since 1975), encouraging rapid increases in consumption. Current tariff levels cover less than two-thirds of operating costs and no capital costs are recovered. Ministry of Electricity calculations of prices and long-run marginal costs suggest that a minimum tariff increase of 75 percent would be needed to cover operational costs and debt service. Prices for kerosene and gas oil are about 20 percent below international prices. In 1984 liquid petroleum gas, used mainly for household cooking, sold for about LS 916 a ton, or about half the refinery cost. Because of subsidies, gas consumption is rising about 15 percent a year, so imports are increasing. The "hidden" subsidy on oil products in 1983 amounted to almost $200 million.

Exchange rate policy and foreign trade

The exchange rate and trading system in Egypt and Syria are complex. The many restrictions that affect trade and external payments include multiple exchange rates, large spreads between buying and selling rates, advance import deposit requirements, and administrative controls on trade flows. Exchange rates are only partially adjusted, so they lag well behind inflation rate differences with trading partners and have been highly overvalued for a long time. Overvalued currencies, together with the excess demand of the early 1980s, have made domestic products increasingly noncompetitive and encouraged the development and expansion of the nontradables sector. The severe shortages of foreign exchange in Egypt and Syria after 1981 called for immediate adjustment policies, but both governments avoided major devaluation and stabilization programs. Instead, they administered more limits on imports and adopted multiple exchange rates, introducing further distortions and inefficiencies.

Jordan maintains a unified and relatively flexible exchange rate, although in recent years it introduced several import restrictions to ease the shortage of foreign exchange. Since 1975, the Jordanian dinar (JD) has been pegged to the IMF's Special Drawing Right (SDR) at a rate of JD 1 = SDR 2.579. Between early 1980 and the end of the first quarter of 1985, when the dollar appreciated against most major currencies, the pegging of the JD to the SDR limited its depreciation against the dollar to 29 percent.

Syria. The rigidity of the Syrian system is exemplified by the official exchange rate, which was fixed at LS 3.925 to the dollar from 1976 until January 1, 1988, when it was depreciated to LS 11.2. Many transactions naturally take place at unofficial rates. And the continuous decline in export competitiveness and the existence of a black market in foreign currency forced the authorities in August 1981 to introduce a parallel rate of LS 5.425 per dollar.

After a deterioration in the balance of payments duing 1982-1987 and an increase in domestic inflation, the Syrian government imposed restrictions and administrative controls on imports and encouraged exports and transfers of private foreign currency. Noninterest bearing monetary deposits were imposed on importers, and a new set of exchange rates were offered to exporters. Nonetheless, the excess demand for foreign currency persisted. By the summer of 1986, the rate on the black market had reached LS 27 per dollar. In early 1987 five principal and two minor exchange rates were in use. During 1987 an effective devaluation took place as various categories of exports were shifted to higher exchange rates.

Beginning in 1988, Syria took a major step toward simplifying the exchange rate system and devaluing the Syrian pound. The exchange rate system was unified to include an official rate (LS 11.2 per dollar), a promotion rate (LS 27 per dollar),[20] and some lower temporary rates for transfers to students overseas and for purchases of airfare.

Egypt. Equally complicated, the exchange rate system in Egypt is fragmented into three pools. The central bank pool handles Suez Canal dues, imports of essential food products and agricultural inputs, and exports of rice, petroleum, raw cotton, and so forth. The exchange rate applied to these transactions was fixed from 1979 until August 1989, when it was depreciated from LE 0.70 to LE 1.10 per U.S. dollar.[21] The commercial bank pool handles mainly workers' remittances, tourism receipts, and certain private sector imports. The exchange rate for these transactions was subject to frequent adjustments and set at LE 0.845 in August 1981, but was reorganized on May 11, 1987, when an initial rate at LE 2.165 was set. The third pool is a legal free market, where rates in this pool are flexible and much lower than in the other two (LE 1.95 to the dollar in October 1986 reaching LE 2.65 in the third quarter of 1989), but imports through the free market are subject to import licensing. The overall real effective exchange rate (the weighted average of the three rates) appreciated 63 percent between January 1982 and March 1985, when the real effective exchange rate index peaked. The main cause of this appreciation was the unchanged nominal exchange rate in the central bank pool, but the other two exchange rates also appreciated. The main effect was to discourage the domestic production of tradables. The industrial and agricultural sectors grew more slowly than the service sector, and nonfuel merchandise exports stagnated or declined in real terms. The heavy subsidization of imports, the complex import control system, and government control of investible resources created an inefficient domestic structure of production, biased toward supplying the domestic market at high cost.

Interest rates and the capital market

Real interest rates in Egypt were negative between 1976 and 1986. Determined administratively, they were not affected by inflation or the demand for credit. This policy encouraged borrowing and led to a distorted pattern of investment, biased toward capital-intensive projects. Interest rates were kept low for such priority sectors as agriculture and industry, but that policy may have hurt rather than helped those sectors—because compressing the supply of funds discouraged the banks from lending to those sectors. Thus those sectors were even more discouraged because agricultural and industrial projects often involve more risk than commercial projects, especially when interest rates are not freely determined and cannot be adjusted to reflect different risk factors for different projects. Moreover, the negative real interest rates in deposits denominated in domestic currency discouraged savings and encouraged both consumption and the accumulation of wealth in foreign currencies.

In both Syria and Egypt the structure and level of interest rates have remained unchanged since 1981, with a ceiling of 9 percent. Priority sectors (based on social and economic considerations) get preferential lending rates. Given the rapid increase in domestic prices, prevailing deposit rates are substantially negative. A 12-month term deposit in Syria, for example, earns 8 percent a year, about a tenth of the 1987 inflation rate.

This government control of the financial markets hampers their efficient functioning and development—as well as the recoveries being attempted in Egypt, Syria, and Jordan. It may help finance the large fiscal deficits and public investment programs in these countries. But this control of interest rates, like the control of product prices, damages the economy by reducing saving rates, making capital markets inefficient, and perpetuating a bias toward investments in projects with low returns.

NOTES

1. Corden and Neary 1982 and van Wijnbergen 1984.
2. The Suez Canal, closed to traffic after 1967, reopened in 1975.
3. In Egypt, which had maintained a balance between agricultural exports and imports in the early 1970s, the trade deficit in agricultural produce had escalated to $2.5 billion by the early 1980s.
4. In Syria and Jordan agricultural output fluctuates because of climate, so it is necessary to average the output for several years as an indicator of the sector's share of GDP.

5. In Jordan, workers' remittances and foreign aid peaked at 40 percent of GDP in the early 1980s, declining to 24 percent in 1986 and 23 percent in 1987.

6. In middle-income developing countries similar to Jordan and Syria, services averaged about 52 percent of GDP in 1985. In lower middle-income countries similar to Egypt, it reached only 47 percent. (World Bank 1987a, pp. 168-69 and 206-07.)

7. As a share of GDP, agriculture declined and services and construction rose—but comparisons are distorted by the steep rise in the petroleum sector's share of GDP. Although agriculture declined relative to other sectors, agricultural output in Egypt grew more than 3 percent a year during the 1970s, while value added grew 8 percent a year in manufacturing and about 11 percent in the service sectors.

8. Arms imports are often financed directly by external grants or loans.

9. In Syria prices rose 60 percent in 1987, while the GDP deflator went up only 39 percent. (World Bank 1989e.)

10. The actual cost of subsidizing goods and services is higher than the recorded cost. Part of the subsidies to petroleum products are not explicitly recorded but are offset against transfers of surpluses from the Syrian Petroleum Company.

11. Converted to U.S. dollars using the official exchange rate.

12. A conservative estimate, considering Syria's system of price controls.

13. IMF data. Source: Egyptian Ministry of Planning.

14. World Bank 1987b.

15. See note 12.

16. The overall medium- and long-term public and publicly guaranteed debt (not including military debt) in 1986 was an estimated $29.7 billion.

17. By our reckoning, the total cost of food subsidies in Egypt was LE 2.3 billion in 1982-1983, LE 2.9 billion in 1983-1984, and LE 2.8 billion in 1984-1985 and 1985-1986.

18. Between 1974 and 1985, Egypt more than doubled its cereal imports, from 3.9 million to 8.9 million metric tons. This made Egypt the world's fourth cereal importer, behind the USSR, Japan, and China. In 1987 Egypt's cereal imports reach 9.3 million tons. (World Bank 1989d.)

19. Even after the increases in energy prices in March 1989, the weighted average of domestic petroleum prices did not exceed 36 percent of world prices and electricity tariffs 24 percent of the long-run marginal cost. (World Bank 1989b, p. 130.)

20. These are the purchase prices for foreign exchange. In the Beirut free market the Syrian pound was traded at 40 to the dollar at the end of 1987.

21. In May 1987 a new flexible bank foreign exchange market was established in an attempt to close the free market outside banks. The commercial bank exchange rate depreciated since May 1987 to LE 2.57 per U.S. dollar in the third quarter of 1989, following developments in the free market rate, to which it is largely pegged.

Table 3.1 Employment by Sector

	Employment 1974		Employment 1981-1982		Distribution of growth in employment	
	(000)	(%)	(000)	(%)	(000)	(%)
Agriculture	4,212	46.6	4,248	36.9	36	1.4
Industry	1,150	12.7	1,487	12.9	337	13.6
Utilities	81	0.9	130	1.1	49	2.0
Construction	315	3.5	700	6.1	385	15.0
Services	3,272	36.2	4,957	43.0	1,675	67.5
Total	9,030	100.0	11,51	100.0	2,482	100.0

Sources: Egypt, Ministry of Planning, and World Bank estimates.

Table 3.2 Revenues, Expenditures and Fiscal Deficits
(percentage of GDP)

	1974-1978	1979	1980	1981	1982	1983	1984	1985	1986	1987
Egypt										
Total revenues	26.8	30.9	45.0	42.4	39.3	37.2	34.8	35.5	28.2	—
Tax revenues	7.6	18.4	22.3	20.6	21.0	19.2	18.2	18.1	15.5	—
Total expenditures	50.2	55.3	61.8	62.5	58.5	60.3	56.8	58.3	45.3	—
Overall deficit	23.4	24.4	16.8	20.1	19.1	23.1	22.0	22.8	17.1	—
External finance	5.7	5.0	3.7	3.9	3.5	3.8	4.7	5.0	3.3	—
Syria										
Total revenues	15.0	23.4	26.5	24.9	27.9	28.9	25.0	25.6	26.2	24.5
Tax revenues	11.9	10.7	10.4	9.9	12.3	12.0	12.6	13.0	14.7	16.1
Total expenditures	49.2	38.8	48.0	40.6	45.4	45.9	46.5	43.6	37.7	31.4
Overall deficit	34.2	15.5	21.4	15.8	17.5	16.9	21.4	18.0	11.5	5.7
External finance	15.9	17.5	11.3	13.0	9.5	9.3	7.2	5.9	3.0	3.0
Jordan										
Total revenues	28.4	24.5	22.7	25.6	27.4	28.2	27.7	27.4	31.3	31.5
Tax revenues	17.0	15.4	13.6	14.2	15.2	15.9	15.5	15.3	14.5	14.4
Total expenditures	65.9	65.5	54.0	51.1	51.1	46.8	44.2	46.1	49.4	50.8
Overall deficit	39.2	40.9	31.4	25.5	23.7	18.6	16.5	18.6	18.1	19.3
External finance	23.1	31.4	27.1	22.2	19.3	18.1	12.8	19.5	14.0	8.0

Source: IMF data and World Bank 1989e.

57

Table 3.3 Summary of Fiscal Operations — Egypt
(in M LE)

	1979	1980	1981	1982	1983	1984	1985	1986	1987
Total revenues	3,684	7,275	8,333	9,749	10,371	11,312	12,792	12,404	—
Tax revenues	2,412	3,997	4,442	5,200	5,363	5,923	6,519	6,837	—
Transfer profits	501	1,756	1,715	2,045	2,075	1,944	2,288	1,924	—
Total expenditures	6,591	9,983	12,272	14,497	16,804	18,476	21,026	19,945	—
Subsidies	1,352	2,166	2,192	2,342	2,876	2,749	2,766	2,295	—
Investment	2,547	3,767	4,671	5,020	5,517	6,544	8,261	6,596	—
Overall deficit	2,907	2,708	3,939	4,748	6,433	7,165	8,234	7,541	—
External financing	628	627	786	858	1,052	1,530	1,796	1,446	—

Table 3.3 Summary of Fiscal Operations — Jordan (cont.)
(in M JD)

	1979	1980	1981	1982	1983	1984	1985	1986	1987
Total revenues	187.9	226.1	309.2	362.2	400.6	415.0	440.8	514.5	531.5
Tax revenues	118.4	136.2	171.3	200.3	225.8	232.2	246.6	238.0	242.4
Transfer profits	24.6	33.2	57.7	73.9	82.9	69.7	82.2	85.3	78.8
Total expenditures	502.2	539.4	616.3	674.7	665.8	663.1	740.4	811.2	857.4
Subsidies	20.6	47.7	37.2	54.4	35.0	46.9	33.5	6.3	6.4
Investment	154.7	177.8	184.7	200.7	176.4	152.5	170.9	199.6	223.1
Overall deficit	314.3	313.3	397.1	312.5	265.2	248.1	299.6	296.8	325.9
External financing	241.0	270.5	267.9	255.1	257.7	191.5	312.8	230.1	134.9

Note: External financing includes foreign grants plus net external borrowing.

Table 3.3 Summary of Fiscal Operations — Syria (cont.)
(in M LS)

	1979	1980	1981	1982	1983	1984	1985	1986	1987
Total revenues	9,202	13,757	16,555	19,202	21,228	18,859	21,266	25,756	30,970
Tax revenues	4,211	5,416	6,588	8,490	8,767	9,501	10,808	14,419	20,362
Transfer profits	61,723	71,173	9,670	9,446	11,732	8,720	9,794	10,193	9,291
Total expenditures	15,284	24,853	27,038	31,218	33,648	35,010	36,288	37,091	38,137
Investment	6,071	9,155	9,863	12,052	12,077	12,110	13,043	12,900	12,417
Overall deficit	6,082	11,096	10,483	12,016	12,420	16,151	15,022	11,335	7,167
External financing	6,883	5,867	8,651	6,534	6,841	5,409	4,932	2,944	5,437

Source: IMF data and World Bank 1989e.

Table 3.4 Egypt - Deficit of Public Enterprises
(as share of GDP)

	1973	1977	1979	1980-81	1981-82	1982-83	1983-84
Public companies	1.2	4.2	6.4	6.2	4.5	4.7	4.1
Economic authorities	2.5	2.1	2.4	-5.9	0.2	2.1	1.4
Total burden	3.7	6.3	8.8	0.2	4.3	6.8	5.5
National fiscal deficit	14.7	16.9	26.9	15.8	25.3	20.6	20.2
Public deficit as a share of national fiscal deficit	25.3	37.0	32.6	1.5	16.8	32.9	30.2

Source: CAPMAS, Ministry of Finance, Egypt and World Bank 1987b.
Note: The dramatic drop in the burden in 1980/81 reflects the increased inflows to the treasury from economic authorities. This increase reflects higher profit transfers (higher petroleum export revenues) and the proceeds from the sale of energy bonds to the public.

Table 3.5 Public Enterprise Exports in Egypt
($US millions)

	1974	1981-1982	1984-1985
Public sector	1,243	5,356	5,279
Petroleum	187	3,329	2,891
Suez Canal		909	897
Other public sector	1,056	1,118	1,491
Private sector	944	1,266	1,564

Source: Central Bank of Egypt.
Note: Exports include goods and nonfactor services. They exclude exports of foreign oil companies.

II
CONSTRAINTS
ON GROWTH

4

HUMAN RESOURCES

Population growth is the single greatest long-term threat to economic development in Egypt and possibly Syria. Other problems include debilitating disease, an inadequately trained labor force, the slow development of new technologies (especially in agriculture), the extremely limited availability of land, the decline in crop yields due to inadequate drainage, the high defense budget, and the dominance of inefficient public enterprises in all sectors of the economy.

POPULATION

The population of the Middle East is growing faster than that of any other region in the world. The population growth rate in Egypt accelerated from 2.5 percent in 1960 to 2.8 percent in 1986. Comparable rates for Syria were 2.9 percent and 3.7 percent, and for Jordan 2.7 percent and 3.2 percent. This growth rate was not steady, however; the growth rate in all three countries experienced an episode of decline. Egypt, especially, had greater hope for further declines in fertility; its growth rate decelerated from 1966 until 1975 and in 1970-1975 averaged only 2.2 percent. But in 1980-1985 the population again grew 2.8 percent a year. In Syria and Jordan the temporary decline was less dramatic. The annual growth rate in Syria fell to 3.3 in 1970-1975 but climbed to 3.6 again in 1980-1985. Comparable rates in Jordan were 3.2 and 3.7, respectively.

Although total fertility rates—the number of babies the average woman will have in her lifetime—have dropped in the last three decades in the three countries, population growth has accelerated. In Egypt the total fertility has declined by 29 percent, in Jordan by 19 percent, and in Syria by 12 percent. Crude birth rates have declined by 19 percent in Jordan, by 17 percent in Egypt, and by 5 percent in Syria, while crude death rates have been more than halved.[1] As public health improves, infant mortality falls, more babies live to grow up, and the population becomes more youthful. The number of women now reaching child-bearing age is larger than ever before, which means many more births than ever before, despite the drop in fertility rates. The World Bank projects that at the end of the century the population of Egypt will be 67.4 million, that of Syria 18 million, and that of Jordan 6 million. Compare these figures with the most recent estimates of 51.5 million for Egypt, 11.7 million for Syria, and 3.9 million for Jordan (including the West Bank).

It might appear that the vast empty spaces in Egypt, Syria, and Jordan could accommodate many more people—and in the long run that may be true—but in the short run high population growth rates impose a heavy burden on these economies. Substantial investments are needed to make agriculture (land) and industry productive enough to support a large population. More resources are needed to provide water, health, and education facilities. The rate at which the capacity to meet essential needs can be increased is not high enough to accommodate the prevailing average family size and rate of population growth in the three countries. Continuing rapid population growth on an even larger base is likely to diminish the quality of life for millions of people in the region. The main cost of such growth, borne principally by the poor, is faltering progress and lost opportunities to improve people's lives.

Rapid population growth in the Middle East slows development in several ways. First, it increases the awkwardness of the choice between higher consumption now and the investment needed to bring higher consumption in the future. Economic growth depends on investment—all the more so if human skills are scarce and technology limited. But if consumption is already low, the resources available for investment are limited; faster population growth makes investment in human capital more difficult. Second, in all three countries population increases threaten the already precarious balance between natural resources and people. The population is still highly dependent on agriculture and the limited potential for increasing production, along with continuing large population increases, condemn many households to continuing poverty. And such increases fuel overuse of limited natural resources, mortgaging the welfare of future generations. Third, rapid population increases make it hard to manage the adjustment that accompanies and promotes economic and social change. And the costs of rapid population growth are cumulative. More births now make it more difficult to slow population growth later, as today's children become tomorrow's new parents. Population policy has a long lead time; in the meantime, other development policies must adapt. Inaction today forecloses options tomorrow, in overall development strategy and future population policy. Worse, inaction today could necessitate more drastic steps tomorrow to slow population growth. Family planning programs are a highly cost-effective way of promoting development and raising living standards.

In all three countries, death rates have fallen sharply as a result of improved health services: in Egypt from 19 per 1,000 in 1965 to 10 in 1985, in Syria from 16 per 1,000 to 8, and in Jordan from 17 per 1,000 to 7 (table 4.1).[2] These are comparable to death rates in the industrial countries. This decline was only somewhat balanced by a moderate decline in the crude birth rate: in Egypt from 43 per 1,000 in 1965 to 36 at present, in Syria from 48 per 1,000 to 45, and in Jordan from 53 per 1,000 to 43. Current crude birth rates, considered almost uniformly high, do not appear to be falling drastically. The total population of the three countries, which rose from 49 million in 1976 to 62.5 million in 1985, will reach 100 million by the turn of the century and will more than double by the year 2010 if present birth rate trends continue.

Although death rates in the three countries have fallen to below 10 per 1,000, the mortality rate is not likely to decline further because more than 45 percent of the population are children under the age of 15 (compared with 37 percent in Asia and 40 percent in Latin America). Africa is the only continent with a similar population/age structure.

As a result, the labor force in Egypt, Syria, and Jordan is growing at a staggering rate: in Egypt at 2.6 percent a year, in Jordan at 4.4 percent a year, and in Syria at 3.5 percent—and these rates are accelerating. Moreover, the urban population—between 46 percent (Egypt) and 69 percent (Jordan) of the total population—is growing 3.5 to 5.5 percent a year. Other developing countries with comparable per capita incomes have similar levels of urbanization but their urban populations are growing much less rapidly.

Jordan has one of the highest population growth rates in the world, and does not have an explicit population policy. The subject has been only indirectly addressed in recent development plans. Limited government involvement reflects the sensitivity of this issue. Child-spacing programs focused on the health of mothers and children have been implemented but it is social development and cultural change that are likely to reduce fertility rates in the longer term.

In contrast, in Egypt the continuing high population growth rate persists despite the government's commitment almost three decades ago to reducing population growth. Egypt has lower fertility and mortality rates than other countries at the same level of per capita GNP —certainly lower than most Arab countries. But the drop in fertility rates has not been sharp enough to ease Egypt's population problem. The data suggest that Egypt's population efforts have not fully succeeded despite continuous program investments. India, on the other hand, another country that has had an intensive long-term population program, has experienced a significant drop in crude birth rates (table 4.1).

Projected consequences for Egypt

To show the long-run implications for Egypt of continued high fertility we will describe the projected consequences of population demand on education, dependency, health care, food supply, and land use under two scenarios. In the first (high-fertility) scenario the total fertility rate (TFR) remains constant at the present 4.6 rate for the next 30 years. In the second (low fertility) scenario, the TFR declines from 4.6 in 1980 to 3.2 in 2000 and then to 2.1 in 2020.[3]

Education. In 1980, 76 percent of children of primary school age (ages 6 to 11) were enrolled in primary school. To maintain this proportion of enrollment under constant TFR, 7.4 million children would be enrolled in primary schools in 2000 and 9.8 million in 2010. If fertility were to decline as assumed in the second scenerio, education costs would be 20 percent lower.

Dependency. A change in fertility would significantly affect the number of people society must support, or the "dependency ratio." Dependency is usually measured by adding the number of people below age 15 and above age 64 and dividing the amount by the number of people aged 15 to 64. The size of the labor force will not be significantly affected by the number of new births during the next 15 years, but the number of dependents to be supported by the labor force will be affected considerably. Assuming a constant TFR by 2010, the number of dependents would be 50 percent higher than if the TFR declined.

Health care. In 1980 Egypt had about 44,000 doctors and 28,000 nurses—or 970 inhabitants per physician and 1,500 inhabitants per nurse. If those ratios were maintained through 2010, Egypt would need 26,200 more physicians and nurses under the high-fertility scenario than if fertility declined.

Food supply. Population growth affects Egypt's ability to meet its food policy objectives. In 1982-1987, the population grew about 2.7 percent a year, so there were about 1.3 million more people to feed every year. Imports of cereals, which provide about half of the average Egyptian's caloric intake, increased. About 3.9 million metric tons of cereals were imported in 1974, increasing to 7.3 million tons in 1981 and 8.8 million tons in 1986.[4] Food production increased by 2.6 percent a year in the five years from 1976 to 1980 and by slightly less in 1981-1986. Total agricultural output increased annually by 2.1 percent in 1965-1974, by 2.6 percent in 1974-1981, by 2.9 percent in 1981-1985, and then dropped to 2.3 percent in 1986-1988.[5] Food production per capita stagnated from 1968 through 1976, then declined by 8 percent from 1977 to 1981. Since 1982 production gradually recovered to regain the per capita level of 1968 in 1987.[6]

Land use. Population density and land use are major development issues in Egypt. In area, Egypt occupies about 1 million square kilometers, 95 percent of which is desert. Close to 42 million of Egypt's more than 50 million inhabitants live within the Nile Valley and Delta in an area measuring 35,000 square kilometers, or 3.5 percent of the country's total area. Population density in this region was 1,200 inhabitants per square kilometer in 1987.[7] If we ignore the possibilities for future land reclamation or increased urbanization, and assume high fertility, 103 million people will reside in the valley and delta by 2020. Only 73 million will populate these areas if we assume declining fertility—more than a 24 percent difference. Increased population density will affect urbanization and poverty levels, will reduce available agricultural land, and will exacerbate social, economic, and health problems. To prevent the negative effects of rapid population growth, policy action to slow down population growth should be more vigorous. Proposals to reduce population growth are sensitive to questions about the proper domain of public policy. At stake in family and fertility issues are the most fundamental human values. In the Middle East, religious beliefs and social norms make it difficult to implement appropriate public policies to reduce fertility. But public policy makes a difference and Egypt's experience with two decades of population policy is encouraging. Many countries have shown that effective measures can be taken to slow population growth.

Each country's policy agenda will depend on its political culture, the nature of the problem it faces, and what it has already accomplished. Affordable measures include the following: public policy to provide alternative ways of securing the benefits that many children provide for their parents, measures to improve educational and income opportunities for women, broader social insurance and pension schemes, policies that encourage breastfeeding and a later marriage age (these reduce population growth by lengthening the average interval between generations), support for family planning programs (making it as easy as possible for individuals to choose the number and timing of their children and helping to close the gap between the number of children parents have and the number they want), and, finally, incentives and disincentives to signal government policy on family size.

POPULATION POLICY IN EGYPT

As early as 1962 Egypt acknowledged that rapid population growth was a major obstacle to economic development. Only in 1965 did it begin to take effective action—by establishing a supreme council for family planning, a family planning board, and by providing family planning services through the Ministry of Health.

Since the early 1970s, Egypt's efforts to accelerate the slowdown in population growth were characterized by attempts to: (a) raise socioeconomic levels, (b) increase educational levels, (c) promote more employment of women, (d) encourage the mechanization of agriculture, (e) industrialize rural areas, (f) reduce infant mortality, (g) increase social security coverage, (h) provide information about the causes and prevention of infant mortality and (g) make family planning services more accessible. The government's program stressed socioeconomic development and deemphasized family planning services.

Demographic and family planning delivery data are too poor in quality to allow precise measurement of the population program's impact. The decline in Egypt's total fertility rate (29 percent between 1960 and 1988)[8] was due in part to a decline in the proportion of married women of childbearing age and to a small drop in marital fertility. This appears to have been accompanied by an increase in the practice of contraception from perhaps less than 5 percent in 1960 to about 21 percent in 1970 and 32 percent in the most recent estimate of women aged 15 to 49.[9]

These relatively poor results and the moderate decline in the birth rate in the past 15 to 20 years (from 39.8 to 35.9) demonstrate that merely providing family planning services is not enough, if people continue to want many children. A stronger political commitment to population control would undoubtedly boost demand for family planning. Such a commitment must also be backed by effective publicity and wider availability of contraceptives at prices most people can afford. Family planning not only helps to prevent unwanted births, but also generally improves the health of women and children. This in turn lowers infant mortality and reduces fears about child survival which keep family size high (Lavy 1985 and Lavy 1986). Family planning measures both satisfy the unmet demand and stimulate the demand for birth control. In many parts of Egypt, as in Jordan and Syria, demand for birth control is low simply because of ignorance about its use and benefits. Private and community organizations have been important in providing family planning services. They can act flexibly and rapidly, are often respected and influential, and can experiment with programs and draw upon extra specialist skills and sources of money. Their activities should be encouraged and, where appropriate, supported by the government and international donors.[10]

Education, especially of women, is critical to reducing population growth. Legal and community action to improve women's general status would also have an impact, mainly by modernizing women's outlook and job prospects in ways that would discourage high fertility. More important are outright systems to deliver family planning and improved services for mothers and children, health services vital for reaching the bulk of the population. All programs aimed at changing people's behavior require continuous contact. To be effective, population and health services require sustained funding, free from short-term budgetary pressures. International donors and others proposing funding assistance should be aware of this.

Health

Despite indications that nutrition and general health have worsened in recent years in Syria and Egypt, overall the three countries have made progress in the health sector. But much needs to be done to alleviate the effects of bad health on the wellbeing of the population. In Egypt life expectancy was 61 years in 1985; in Jordan and Syria it was 64. In all three countries, life expectancy had risen from a low 50 years in 1965. The life expectancy gap between these countries and that in industrial countries (79 years in 1985) has narrowed, but other serious health problems remain. This is especially true of infant mortality, which in the industrial world ranges from 6 per 1,000 births in Denmark to 12 in 1,000 in Italy. In Egypt it is 93, in Syria 54, and in Jordan 49 per 1,000 births. The death rate for children 1 to 4 is close to zero in the industrial world but 11 per 1,000 in Egypt.

As in the rest of the world after 1945, the mortality rate in Egypt, Syria, and Jordan appeared to decline because of: (a) higher levels of education generally, (b) wider access to better medical services, and (c) the virtual elimination of widespread famine, epidemic and endemic disease because of improved transportation systems, better food distribution, immunization campaigns, and the introduction of DDT. These countries made important strides in these areas in the last three decades—except in rural areas, where everyone, but women in particular, have less access to markets, health services, and education than the urban population. The higher mortality rates in rural areas can be reduced by expanding services to rural communities.

The mortality rate has declined but serious health problems remain in these countries. The major causes of death in Egypt are the same now as they were in 1937, although at lower levels. Diseases of the digestive and respiratory systems still account for about half of all deaths. Schistosomiasis, poliomyelitis, and measles continue to be major health problems. (Some progress has been made with tuberculosis, cholera has been brought under control, and smallpox has been eradicated.) The high death rate from digestive and respiratory illnesses and the persistence of diseases such as measles and polio that immunization could prevent suggest that Egypt's health service delivery system is not functioning optimally. Much more can be done, especially in preventive medicine, to improve health conditions in Egypt.

The rapid decline in Jordan's mortality rate in the past two decades reflects both improved living conditions and better health care. As a result Jordan now exhibits a mixed pattern of morbidity and mortality—the chronic disease profile of an industrialized country is increasingly superimposed on the infectious disease pattern typical of developing countries. Diarrhea and respiratory diseases are the most common causes of illness and death in children under five. It is unclear to what extent malnutrition contributes to infant and child mortality but the nutritional status of infants and children has improved significantly in the last decade.

The pattern of infant and child mortality suggests ways to decrease them further. Symptoms of diarrhea are related to contaminated water and poor hygiene, so high priority must be given to better water, sanitation, and health education. Child survival in Jordan could also be improved substantially by child spacing. Recent analysis of the World Fertility Survey data shows that when the birth interval was more than four years, 48 out of 1,000 children died before the age of five, compared to 89 out of 1,000 when the interval was less than two years. About three out of five births in Jordan are supervised by health professionals; the rest are delivered by traditional dayahs, relatives, or friends. Further decreases in infant and maternal mortality are likely to result from improved prenatal and obstetrical care.

For adults the main causes of death are heart and circulatory disease, respiratory disease, and cancer. Overall, Jordan is well prepared, by virtue of its resources and well-developed infrastructure, to launch a preventive campaign against these major causes of adult mortality. Such an approach would be less costly and more effective than providing curative and rehabilitative care.

The data on morbidity in Jordan are incomplete, and the following findings only tentative. Diarrhea and respiratory diseases clearly account for much illness at all ages. Diseases preventable by immunization are less prevalent but still occur. Most parasitic diseases are not thought to be a major problem. Only imported cases of malaria occur, and schistosomiasis is confined largely to Egyptian and other migrant laborers. Overall, the morbidity pattern is typical of a middle-income country.

A recent World Bank report recommended the following goals for Jordan's health sector: improving access to and assuring the quality of health care and containing costs. Improving access means identifying unserved, underserved, and high-risk population groups and removing physical and financial barriers to basic health care services. Cost containment requires new mechanisms to calculate and reduce unit costs, and to examine who pays health care costs.

Better health and nutrition are not only humanitarian imperatives. They are also basic requirements for sustained economic growth and slower population growth rates. Poor health reduces a person's productivity and impairs a child's learning ability. The current health care systems in Egypt, Syria, and Jordan do not meet the health needs of their people. These systems have emphasized urban health care, particularly through ill-equipped hospitals with highly trained medical staff. The rural areas are correspondingly neglected and preventive treatment is limited. People in some parts of Syria and Egypt have no access to health services at all. In some parts of these countries procurement and distribution of drugs and supplies is inefficient, services are erratic and unstable, medical education is inappropriate, and health workers are badly supported and supervised.

Access to safe water supplies also affects health. Recently rural water supply programs have been encouraged but maintenance has been a great problem. Urban water and sanitation systems have also suffered from neglect and population pressure.

INVESTMENT IN HUMAN CAPITAL

Education is critical to the development of a productive population. Indeed, research shows that education may be the best investment in improving health and nutrition (and reducing fertility) in developing countries. The widespread development and adoption of new technologies will also require a better educated population. Syria, for example, sees the need to upgrade the educational level and skills of its labor force as fundamental to its development plan. The Syrian government is committed to the equal distribution of educational services to its people.

Jordan's development plans emphasize the establishment of an education and training program that will generate the human resources needed to sustain its industrial development strategy and reduce its dependence on foreign labor. Improved access to education in Jordan since 1975 is a direct result of the government's strong commitment to human resource development. Enrollments have increased about 30 percent at the primary level, 88 percent at the preparatory level, and 178 percent at the secondary level. School enrollment of women, which in 1975 was already higher than in other Middle Eastern countries, rose even more later. Since 1975 female enrollment as a percentage of total enrollment has risen from 46 to 48 percent at the primary level, from 43 to 46 percent at the preparatory level, and from 37 to 46 percent at the secondary level. Recently Jordan has established general vocational secondary schools and has developed prevocational courses in preparatory and secondary schools.

Egypt's labor force, by contrast, suffers from illiteracy and low skill levels. For example, 51 percent of the work force was illiterate in 1980 and another 23 percent could only read and write a little. Despite the government's sustained efforts over two decades to expand education, Egypt's educational and training system needs great improvement. Efforts should be directed at improving the quality of basic education and expanding secondary technical education. Such fundamental improvements are hampered by the government's bias toward higher education. Many resources are diverted to higher education at the expense of the basic school system. In the government's 1982-1987 fiscal plan, 53 percent of education and training investments were earmarked for higher education, 34.5 percent for primary, intermediate, and secondary education, and the rest for vocational training. Egypt's bias toward higher education—manifested further in guarantees of government jobs for graduates in certain areas—must be corrected if Egypt is to give all its citizens basic education and skills.

NOTES

1. World Bank 1989a.
2. See World Bank 1989a, pp. 90, 160, 300.
3. Ibid.
4. More than 9.3 million tons is the most recent estimate by the World Bank. Ibid., p. 91.
5. World Bank 1989b, p. 132.
6. World Bank 1989e, pp. 238-39.
7. Agricultural land density (total population per square kilometer of agricultural land), increased from 1,100 some 25 to 30 years ago to 1,960 in the most recent estimate. World Bank 1989a, p. 90.
8. Ibid.
9. Ibid.

10. In most of the third world, foreign aid has met roughly half the cost of family planning policies. China has paid all the cost of its birth control program (around $1 a head) itself and India four-fifths of its program. *The Economist* January 20, 1990, p. 26.

Table 4.1 Demographic Indicators

	Egypt	Zambia	India	Bolivia	Indonesia	Tunisia	Syria	Jordan	Libya
GNP per capita (1985 dollars)	610	390	260	470	530	1,190	1,570	1,560	7,170
Crude birth rate									
1965	44	51	44	46	44	47	47	47	49
1985	36	49	33	42	32	32	44	39	45
Crude death rate									
1965	20	24	20	22	23	19	18	20	19
1985	10	15	12	19	12	9	8	7	10
TFR	4.7	6.8	4.5	6.3	4.1	4.6	6.7	6.2	7.2

Source: The World Bank, *World Development Report*, various years.

5

THE TRADABLES

ENCOURAGING AGRICULTURAL GROWTH

The agricultural sector in Syria, Jordan, and Egypt faces increasing constraints on long-term growth. Many of the constraints are a result of almost three decades of central planning and the associated land allotments of crop production, the fixing of both producer and consumer prices, and the establishment of state production farms (mainly in Syria and Egypt). Here we focus on the most important constraints and the needed policy reforms.

Egypt

Agricultural growth accelerated sharply in the 1970s, as a result of the cumulative benefits of the Aswan Dam and the introduction of high-yielding varieties; it stagnated in the 1980s. Several factors constrain the long-term growth of Egyptian agriculture: poor drainage; institutional weaknesses in applied research, extension, and marketing; the dearth of available land; and the inability of large public investments in new lands to add significantly to the productive base. Egypt has taken steps to resolve some of these constraints, but not always successfully. Since 1973 the government has invested considerably in a comprehensive drainage system, but more than half of the government's investments in agriculture are directed at land reclamation. Past large public land reclamation schemes have suffered from poor management and design, insufficient auxiliary services, and uncritical selection of reclamation sites. There is little evidence that future land reclamation efforts would fare better. Expenditures earmarked for the rehabilitation of the Nile barrages and the Aswan Dam are also disproportionately high at a time when the share of public investment allocated to agriculture in the fiscal budget is smaller than ever.

Emphasis should shift from efforts to expand horizontally through land reclamation to vertical development through intensified production on land already under cultivation. Investment should be directed at improving and extending drainage, rehabilitating and modernizing the irrigation system, and providing adequate maintenance so both irrigation and drainage will operate effectively. The physical works and the operating efficiency of the water coverage and distribution system also need substantial improvements at all levels. Sizable investments are needed in drainage and irrigation and are likely to yield significant rates of return.

The support services of extension, research, and marketing should be reorganized to provide farmers with timely, tested advice on raising yields and efficiently marketing output. The Ministry of Agriculture has begun to revitalize research, extension, seed, credit, and agricultural mechanization services, but these efforts must be vigorously extended. Improving these services should not involve heavy capital investment, but would require some funds and basic organizational changes.

All these changes should make farms and farmers more efficient and productive and should improve the quality and diversity of Egypt's agricultural products—which is important for exports. Egypt's favorable climate and low labor costs should put it at an advantage in supplying Europe with winter fruits and vegetables. But Egypt does not yet have the infrastructure and quality standards it needs to capture the European market. The government should develop the facilities it needs for a modern, diversified, export-oriented agricultural sector and for reducing its dependence on cotton exports.

Part of the solution to the stagnation and poverty in rural Egypt may be to reduce the size of the agricultural population, which is much too large for the amount of cultivated land. More than 35 percent of Egypt's people earns their living in agriculture, on only 25 million acres. Yet agriculture as a share of GDP is only 18 percent—so the average income of the Egyptian farmer is only half the per capita GDP.

Syria

Agricultural production in Syria depends highly on weather conditions, as only about 17 percent of farmlands are irrigated.[1] The rainfed sector predominates, so agricultural output has fluctuated considerably in recent years. The drought in 1984 brought a 12-percent decline in total production. Production of wheat and barley, grown mostly in the rainfed sector, fell 34 percent and 71 percent, respectively, and lentils, 40 percent. Inadequate rainfall in early spring 1987 again reduced the output of cereals. Wheat production declined 17 percent and barley, 49 percent.

For agriculture to develop in Syria, irrigation must expand to mitigate the effects of poor weather conditions. In 1975 the Syrian government undertook the Euphrates Basin land reclamation project, with the aim of doubling the irrigated area. Another irrigation project is under way at Haran, aimed at irrigating 30 to 50 thousand hectares. Progress on these projects has been slow because of technical difficulties and foreign exchange constraints.

Jordan

The growth of the agricultural sector—only a small part of Jordan's economy—has been constrained by technological problems.[2] Most important, Jordan does not have the high-quality system of research and extension that is needed to help farmers find timely solutions to sophisticated farming problems. One way such a research system could help is to find ways to increase productivity and lower the costs of production in rainfed areas, where production of cereals, pulses, and red meat fluctuates greatly and has not expanded. Other countries have experienced success with, and there are international research institutions that specialize in, dryland agriculture. Jordanian research institutions could tap these organizations for assistance or collaboration.

Jordan also needs to improve its water management and irrigation systems. Piped and drip irrigation still cover only part of the irrigated areas and should be extended further. Water-use fees are low in the Jordan valley and should be raised, if for no other reason than to encourage farmers to invest in the equipment needed to manage the water more efficiently.

Jordan's agricultural sector should take advantage of its proximity to the newly rich oil countries. In recent years, Jordan has exported $60

million to $70 million worth of agricultural products a year to these
countries, by land. Jordan could expand these exports by specializing
in the export products—especially fresh vegetables, poultry, and dairy
products—that are in demand in Saudi Arabia and the other Gulf states.
   Jordan and Syria should also adopt Egypt's practice of encouraging
foreign investment. Foreign investors could help introduce these
countries to the new technologies, advanced management practices, and
modern marketing methods they need to modernize the industrial sector
and increase economic efficiency.

REVITALIZING INDUSTRY

   Because of their political orientation, the industrial sector in Egypt,
Syria, and to some extent Jordan has been developed by the public
sector. All major manufacturing activities have been undertaken by the
public sector, the private sector has been limited to small plants, and the
traditional sector has played a secondary role. Theoretically, foreign
participation has been allowed, but there have been few practical
instances.
   Modern manufacturing is limited, having stagnated at about 15 percent
of GDP and 12 percent of employment between 1965 and 1987. Most
industries are isolated from world markets and new technology, and
operate at higher cost than operations elsewhere. Protectionism and
public sector monopolies have discouraged the innovation that increases
productivity and the export growth needed to finance import
requirements. These countries must stimulate private sector initiatives
and shift industry toward high-growth, competitive enterprises that are
linked to the world economy.
   A first step in integrating private sector participation in industry would
be to end the preferential treatment given to public enterprises in access
to credit, inputs, and foreign exchange. Second, the governments in
Egypt and Jordan, especially, must streamline controls on private
investment and licensing. Third, and most important, the governments
must create a more stable, more predictable economic environment.
Uncertainty about exchange and interest rates is widespread, and the
laws and procedures governing investment change frequently—so many
private investors have adopted a "wait and see" policy. To regain the
confidence of the private sector, all three governments must prepare,

announce, and follow through by implementing a detailed reform program.

They should also develop new industrialization strategies—putting less emphasis on expanding industrial capacity and more emphasis on developing human, technological, and institutional capabilities. The most successful newly industrialized countries, while protecting local markets, have opened them to competition, provided export incentives, and identified the educational needs and technical skills that build a flexible labor force. In Egypt, Syria, and Jordan, this would mean a shift from regulation to competition, from central planning to a market orientation, and from attempts to transplant technology to the systematic building up of domestic capabilities. Can such policies work in the Middle East? Yes, if the private sector's export response to recent policy changes in Syria is any evidence. Between 1985 and 1988, private exports in Syria jumped from $140 million to $440 million in response to the government's relaxation of controls and the opportunities for profit created by a more realistic exchange rate.[3]

REFORMING PUBLIC ENTERPRISES

The public sector's share in total productive assets has grown large in Egypt and Syria. The energy, industry, transport, and financial sectors are dominated by public firms. Even in agriculture, public investment is heavy—in irrigation, land reclamation, agricultural marketing, and even direct production of agricultural commodities. Thus public financing places a heavy burden on the Syrian and Egyptian budgets. More important, much of the public sector is economically inefficient because of interrelated problems that have no easy solutions: poor management, cumbersome organization, distorted pricing, outmoded technology, lack of autonomy, labor problems, poor financial performance and, especially in Syria, inadequate access to imports.

Any economic reform program must eliminate the constraints on growth associated with these public entities. Most important, reform of public enterprises must include more flexible pricing. By making public enterprise operations and investments self-financing, better pricing can reduce their share of the public deficit. Price flexibility facilitates the pursuit of sound public finance policies. It alleviates pressure on the government to raise taxes (often costly in terms of administration and economic distortions) and to raise financing through inflation, crowding out, and foreign debt. Price controls distort incentives. Flexible pricing would correct those distortions and allow for efficient management and resource allocation—provided prices or user charges reflect true costs. On internationally traded goods, international prices are generally an appropriate reference point. For output not traded internationally—power, water, and telecommunications, for example—the long-run marginal cost of production should be the basis for pricing. Underpricing leads to overexpanded capacity, unnecessary burdens on government budgets, and excessive foreign borrowing. Utilities are often underpriced because cumbersome centralized mechanisms for revising utility tariffs delay price increases after costs have gone up. Political difficulties can cause further delay. Some countries overcome these problems through small but frequent price increases.

The second major goal of reform should be operational autonomy for managers. Public enterprise managers should have full flexibility about labor, wages, and other incentives, and a greater say in investment decisions. Of course, improved performance requires a balance between autonomy and accountability, which requires continuous monitoring of performance. That is difficult when the number of public enterprises and parent ministries is large, as it is in Egypt and Syria. To evaluate a wide range of public enterprises—utilities, manufacturing enterprises, transport companies, marketing boards, and financial institutions—requires skill and resources not often available outside the enterprises themselves. To ensure accountability and improvements, public enterprises should accept competition from and the involvement of the private sector.

A third goal of reform should be to ensure financial self-reliance so government assistance can be eliminated. Setting prices based on economic costs will go a long way toward limiting the need for both central government transfers and public enterprise borrowing. To keep them financially viable, public enterprises should be explicitly reimbursed from the budget for the cost of financially inviable but socially desirable projects. The costs and benefits of such subsidies should be evaluated by standard investment criteria. In some instances it may be more effective to subsidize low-income consumers by charging them less than cost and charging higher-income consumers more. Rather than be subsidized, public enterprises should peg taxes just as private enterprises do. This will put them on an equal footing with private competitors and encourage efficiency.

Finally, private sector involvement could make public enterprise operations more efficient and reduce their drain on fiscal resources. Privatization is broadly defined as increased private sector participation in the management and ownership of activities and assets controlled and owned by the government. More than 50 developing countries have begun to reduce the administration and financial burden of the public sector by liberalizing and streamlining public enterprises. Full and rapid privatization is not possible in Egypt and Syria, and the barriers to such a change in Jordan are significant, but intermediate solutions—such as subcontracting, leasing, or allowing private competition—may be feasible.

NOTES

1. Agrigulture's share in GDP amounted in recent years to 20 percent of GDP and to 30 percent of total employment. Thus average income in the agricultural sector is about two thirds of per capita GDP.
2. In recent years, 8 to 9 percent of GDP and 10 percent of total employment. Average income in agriculture is close to the national average.
3. Central Bank of Syria and IMF data.

6

DEFENSE'S DRAIN ON GROWTH AND DEVELOPMENT

The massive military build-up in Egypt, Syria, and Jordan in the four decades after World War II has few parallels, especially among small, poor economies. By the early 1980s total military spending was 25 percent of GNP in Syria, 18 percent in Jordan, and more than 12 percent in Egypt. In Israel, covered here because of the direct link between its military build-up and that in Egypt, Jordan, and Syria, the corresponding ratio was 25 percent. Compare these ratios with a range of 2 to 4 percent in most other developing countries, and with an average of 4.5 percent in the Organization for Economic Cooperation and Development (OECD) countries.[1] The massive military spending in Egypt, Syria, and Jordan has been possible only through the appropriation of enormous domestic resources and the granting of similarly enormous external aid, either by the United States, the Soviet Union or the rich Arab oil states.

These exceedingly high shares of military spending in economic activity raise questions about whether such spending contributes to growth and development—or saps it. And these questions raise others about how best to measure this spending, and make cross-country comparisons, especially when only a part of it is recorded and that part is measured in local currencies whose official rates depart from market rates. In this chapter we begin by suggesting a way of estimating military spending. We then explore the relationship between military spending and economic growth and development—finding that other studies showing a positive relationship have little bearing here because they are inapplicable average results for countries with very low ratios of military spending to GNP. We conclude by assessing the changes in the three countries' military spending as they plunged from boom to stagnation—forcing them into the de-facto disarmament in the 1980s.

ESTIMATING MILITARY SPENDING

Estimating the amounts and trends of military spending in Egypt, Syria, and Jordan on the basis of official data is difficult. The first problem is that such data are incomplete. None of these countries records all military spending in their budgetary allocations. Arms imports and outlays for servicing external military debt are excluded from budgetary and balance of payments statistics as are a part of military capital expenditures. Moreover, in Egypt and Syria, spending for internal security is excluded from the defense budget. The officially reported military spending may thus cover only current domestic defense spending. A second problem relates to selecting an appropriate conversion factor for cross-country comparisons, made more complex with the emergence of multiple exchange rates and their divergence from market rates.

What, then, of other estimates of military spending? Several international agencies and institutions regularly publish estimates and even time series of military expenditures for many countries. Generally these estimates are based on official sources, sometimes adjusted if official data are considered to be partial, as with Egypt, Syria, and Jordan. The most comprehensive published estimates of military spending are in the annual volumes of the U.S. Arms Control and Disarmament Agency (ACDA) on world military expenditures and arms transfers.[2] But none of these publications has overcome the problem of incomplete information and inadequate conversion factors. Further flawing their estimates are problems of pricing arms imports and distinguishing between supply agreements and actual payments and delivery dates.

Here are some examples of why the ACDA's estimates of military expenditures in Egypt, Syria, and Jordan (as well as Israel) are questionable. Its report of 1987 put Jordan's arms imports in 1981-1983 at a figure that exceeded total military spending more than 60 percent—obviously inconceivable. It put Syria's arms imports in 1980-

1982 at 10 percent more than total military spending. Moreover, total military spending minus arms imports should equal domestic defense spending, which is estimated to be ridiculously low in certain years in Syria, as well as fluctuating by hundreds of percentage points. And while Israel's balance of payments statistics are considered to be reasonably reliable, in the years 1982-1985 officially reported arms imports were almost twice as large than those in ACDA's report of 1987. The implied import component in ACDA's report of Israel's total military spending in 1983-1985 is only 8 to 9 percent, amazingly low for a country relying so heavily on military imports.[3]

Because published estimates of military spending trends in Egypt, Syria, and Jordan are so unreliable, we calculated our own. We believe that such spending is best estimated by using budgetary defense allocations deflated by an overall GDP price deflator (table 6.1). (Since a specific military spending—or public expenditures—deflator is not available, the overall GDP deflator is used.) The obvious weakness of this rough estimate is the exclusion of arms imports. To compensate for this exclusion we assume that arms imports represent a constant 40 percent of military spending during 1980-1987 (table 6.2). The advantage of this approach is that it avoids the need to estimate yearly arms imports from partial and uncertain data. Another is that it avoids the distortionary effects of fluctuating exchange rates. Taking into account only changes in domestic prices, the approach also smoothes wide annual fluctuations in arms imports, fluctuations that disturb analysis of trends in total military expenditures.

The approach suggested here relies on the coverage of reported official defense outlays and on the relevance of the assumed share of arms imports in military spending. If officially recorded defense outlays are a close approximation of actual domestic military expenditures in Egypt, Syria, and Jordan, rough estimates based on defense allocations deflated by the GDP price deflator can be a reasonable indicator of the levels and trends of military spending. Our assumption of a constant share of arms imports in military spending is based on experience that the share does not change dramatically in the short run, except for occasional fluctuations.

The share that we use in our calculations here is 40 percent, based on the actual average of 37 percent in Israel during 1982-1987, a figure widely believed to be similar to that in Egypt, Syria, and Jordan. All four countries have modern armies equipped with sophisticated imported weapons. Military-industrial production is more developed in Israel, and the supply of domestically produced military equipment is probably more significant—which would imply a relatively lower ratio. But the armies in the three Arab states are probably less capital intensive, which would make them less likely to have a much higher ratio. We must emphasize that our estimates are based on partial reported data and therefore deserve cautious treatment—more as indicators of trends and orders of magnitude than as accurate figures. We nevertheless hope that they can shed some quantitative light on the economic burdens of the arms race in the three countries.

Levels of Military Spending

The most striking feature of the military build-up in Egypt, Syria, and Jordan (as well as in Israel) is its size, duration, and intensity (tables 6.2 and 6.3). From a relatively modest 6 percent of GNP in the mid-1950s, armament outlays grew rapidly during the next 20 years in Egypt, Syria, and Israel until the war of 1973. They continued to accelerate in Syria and Jordan until the boom's end in 1982. In Egypt the pace of rearmament leveled off after 1973, following disengagement agreements and a peace treaty with Israel. The share of military spending in GNP declined from 18 percent in 1972 to 11.5 percent in 1979. In both Syria and Israel the share grew continuously to a peak of some 25 percent in 1979. In Jordan, the share was already very high in the mid-1950s. The Jordanian economy was then small, and the Arab Legion, supported by Britain, relatively large. After the withdrawal of British involvement and military support in 1956, the share of military spending in GNP declined somewhat and later leveled off in the range of 15 to 16 percent. These extremely high ratios reflect a continuous (and large) military build-up, requiring enormous domestic and foreign currency resources.[4]

Favorable economic conditions and massive external aid enabled Syria and Jordan to accelerate the pace of rearmament between 1973 and 1982. Military spending in Egypt, on the other hand, did not increase at all in real terms between 1974 and 1979. Instead, Egypt directed more resources to development and the well-being of its population. As a result, Egypt lost its position as the dominant military power in the group of confrontation states. Its share of military spending in that group declined from 70 percent in 1972 to 46 percent in 1979 and less than 40 percent in 1986 (table 6.4).

Because of mounting economic constraints in the early 1980s, the pace of armament slowed in Egypt, Syria, and Jordan between 1982 and 1987. The downturn was most conspicuous in Syria. There, following an average annual growth in military spending of 14.5 percent from 1973 to 1982, military spending did not increase at all from 1982 to 1985. With its economic performance deteriorating further between 1986 and 1988, Syria cut domestic military spending significantly to stabilize its economy and improve its shaky balance of payments position (tables 6.3 and 6.5 and figure 6.1). Syria's economic difficulties are squeezing military spending. And the Soviet Union seems to be taking a tougher position on new equipment sales. Moscow is reportedly insisting that Syria begin making payments on its estimated $15 billion in military debt.

In Egypt, after a seven-year freeze, military spending rose rapidly—18 percent a year—between 1980 and 1983 (table 6.5) as a result of improved external economic circumstances and U.S. military aid. But recurrent balance of payments crises after 1982, together with debt arrears and domestic inflationary pressures, forced Egypt to cut military spending. After leveling off in 1984 and 1985, domestic military spending was cut almost 10 percent in real terms in 1986 to 1987. Egypt's military spending as a percentage of GNP declined from 12.5 percent in 1982 to 10.5 percent in 1986.

Economic crises also forced the Jordanian government to slow the pace of growth in military spending, although less so than in Syria and Egypt. Military spending grew only 1.8 percent in 1983 and 3.5 percent in 1984, far less than the average of 10 percent a year between 1973 and 1982 (tables 6.3 and 6.5). Despite the continuing deterioration in economic conditions, growth in military spending shot up again in 1985 and 1986, before cuts in military spending in real terms of 2.5 percent in 1987 and 3.5 percent in 1988. The resurgence in 1985 and 1986 seems curious in view of the continuing deterioration in economic conditions in Jordan—and should thus be interpreted cautiously.

From 1984 to 1986, Israel cut more than 8 percent of domestic military spending in an effort to reduce its fiscal deficit and triple-digit inflation, as part of a comprehensive stabilization program. The cost of dealing with the Palestinian uprising in Gaza and the West Bank has created pressure for more military spending, but ministers now accept that the economy cannot be reformed without cutting back on the defense burden. In addition, U.S. aid has begun to decline in real terms.

It seems that the build-up in military spending in the region took a life of its own as one country responded to perceived increases in the threat of the other. The arms race was stimulated by favorable economic circumstances and rising external aid. But circumstances drastically changed after 1982 with the deterioration of economic conditions and the contraction of military aid. Add to this the rapprochement between the two superpowers—the major suppliers of sophisticated weapons and military aid—and the spirit of military spending has turned downward.

Economic Burdens

The rapid expansion and enormous levels of military spending in Egypt, Syria, and Jordan seriously constrain their growth. Immense resources have been allocated and wasted in the region's recurrent wars and ongoing arms race. The structural balance of all three economies has deteriorated because of inflated budgetary spending, large fiscal deficits, increased money supply, and domestic and external borrowing to finance the deficits. All this has discouraged exports, hindered the diversification of production, and contributed to the rising share of the nontradable sectors—making each of these economies more vulnerable to external shocks.

A commonly accepted indicator of the economic burden of defense spending is the ratio of military spending to GNP. But external military aid has been massive for Egypt, Syria, Jordan, and Israel, making the ratio of domestic military spending to GDP a better indicator of the economic burden of defense in these countries.

On top of ordinary economic aid, Egypt has received in recent years annual military grants from the U.S. government amounting to $1.2 billion—and Israel $1.8 billion.[5] These grants probably finance the greater part of arms imports (table 6.6). Previously, military aid to both countries comprised special military loans, supplemented by much smaller grants. To alleviate the heavy burden of servicing these loans on the balance of payments, the U.S. government substituted grants for loans.

To support their military efforts, Syria and Jordan receive external aid from the rich Arab oil states, but the amount of specific military aid has never been disclosed. Unofficial information in the world press in recent years has also referred to arms deals between the Soviet Union and Syria, financed by the Arab oil states. Official data have never been disclosed on such transactions, or on the external financing of Jordan's arms imports. It is generally believed that a part of Soviet arms were supplied to Syria on credit terms, resulting in a substantial military external debt whose amounts and terms have never been disclosed. Unofficial press reports peg Syria's debt to the Soviet Union at $15 billion—and refer to Jordan's agreements with several Western countries for the supply of arms on credit.

Although the precise amounts, or even rough estimates, of specific military grants to Syria and Jordan are not available, it seems probable that Syria and Jordan (like Israel and Egypt) had early on to finance their arms imports from their own resources, either cash payments or military loans. But in more recent years, as foreign debts rose and sophisticated weapons became prohibitively expensive, specific military grants are financing a growing share of arms imports. This pattern, too, makes the share of domestic military spending in GDP a better indicator of the defense burden (table 6.7).[6]

That is extremely high in both Syria and Jordan. It fluctuated in the range of 14 to 15 percent in Syria during 1982-1985, declining to 13 percent in 1986. It remained more or less stable in Jordan at 14 to 15 percent during 1982-1987. And it averaged 14.5 percent in Israel during 1982-1984, dropping to 11.7 percent in 1985-1987.[7] These ratios are much higher than anywhere else in the world. In Egypt the share of domestic military spending declined sharply after the 1973 war. A freeze on domestic defense outlays until 1979, coupled with a sharp rise in rates of economic expansion, was reflected in a decline of the ratio from about 11 percent in 1972 to only 6.5 percent in 1980. It rose to more than 8 percent during 1981-1985 and then declined to 7.1 percent in 1986 and 6.8 percent in 1987. But even this lower ratio constitutes a heavy burden on Egypt's poor economy, especially when compared with most other developing countries, for which the defense burdens generally are 2 to 4 percent of GNP.[8]

Defense spending represented an astonishing 55 percent to 65 percent of total public consumption in Jordan and Syria in 1985-1987 and more than 70 percent in Syria in 1980-1984, crowding out social and economic services (table 6.7). In Egypt, domestic defense spending as a percentage of total public consumption is lower than in Syria and Jordan, but at 44 percent in 1986 it was still among the highest in the world. Domestic defense spending in Israel was 41 percent of total public consumption in 1985-1987. That left little for social development. Education claimed only 9 percent of central government expenditures in Syria, 12 percent in Egypt, and 14 percent in Jordan—and health a mere 1 percent in Syria and 4 percent in Jordan.[9]

MILITARY SPENDING AND ECONOMIC DEVELOPMENT

The economic effects of domestic military spending are similar to other public outlays demanding labor and other resources. There are some positive spinoffs of such spending on the civilian economy in developing countries, such as those from R&D, modernization, and managerial experience. But such spinoffs probably do not outweigh the wide range of direct and indirect negative effects. These negative effects include depriving resources from investments, imposing higher tax rates on productivity, inflationary financing of budgetary deficits, sacrificing savings and the balance of payments, and so on.

Emile Benoit, in his well-known work of 1978, attempted to establish that military spending has a positive effect on economic growth in developing countries—that is, that it stimulates their economic growth.[10] His conclusion is based on a positive relation between the defense burden ratios and rates of economic growth, derived from a statistical analysis of a large sample of 44 developing countries. Benoit's astonishing findings have elicited much criticism, one of the more comprehensive ones by Deger.[11] Deger argues that if account is taken of the various other channels through which defense spending directly and indirectly affects growth (she terms it the "mobilization of resources effect"), the overall effect of military spending is negative.[12] She further argues that a cross-section of countries may yield different results from Benoit's if the less developed countries (LDCs) were subgrouped "into suitable groups so that they have common characteristics in stages of development".[13]

Deger's approach seems more plausible. We doubt whether Benoit's results are at all relevant to the economic situation in Egypt, Syria, Jordan, and Israel in more recent times.[14] These four states have reached record levels of defense burdens, and their economies have been characterized most recently by large fiscal deficits, huge foreign debts, domestic and external imbalances, biases toward nontradable sectors, and numerous
other distortions and resource misallocations. It therefore seems implausible to suggest in such circumstances that expanded defense

spending would promote economic growth. Instead, the recommendation would be just the opposite.

All four countries have recently taken steps to curb military spending with an objective to stabilize their economies, despite the high priority they attach to defense. These unusual steps are also aimed at promoting the structural transformation that is crucial for sustained growth. Exceptional external conditions and massive foreign aid enabled the prolonged enormous military build-up and rapid economic growth of these countries during the boom. Today, after the boom's end, the weight of the defense burden has become evident.

Heavy military spending, beyond a certain level, becomes intolerable in poor developing countries, precisely because it is inimical to growth. When domestic defense spending uses 50 percent or more of total public consumption, it unleashes instabilities and imbalances in the economy. Unless cut back, military spending will frustrate—even doom—any attempt to eliminate large fiscal deficits. Cutbacks in military spending are also crucial for reducing the size of the public sector, an important measure to stimulate the expansion of tradable sectors. Further, extremely large domestic expenditures on defense (10 to 15 percent of GDP) deprive resources from essential social and economic services and crowd out private investments. They reduce government savings, increase current account deficits, boost foreign and domestic public debts, run up the money supply, and thus undermine the effectiveness of macroeconomic policies.

When the balance of payments worsens and inflationary pressures increase, governments generally tighten direct import controls and increase subsidies, intensifying the price distortions and hurting resource allocation and productivity. Such distortionary effects of heavy military burdens—together with high tax rates and high interest rates, such as those in Israel—aggravate poor economic performance and limit long-term growth opportunities. Thus, the extremely high ratios of military spending in the GDP of Egypt, Syria, Jordan, and Israel inevitably absorb untenable amounts of available resources and reduce the standard of living of the population—unless foreign aid is large. The fact that defense spending has recently declined in these countries unmasks the economic stringencies of too heavy a defense burden.

How much can the worsening economic performance of all four states be attributed to heavy defense burdens or to other factors? The question is impossible to answer in numerical terms. But military spending has been so immense that it has been tying up resources that could instead be used to promote growth. With military spending accounting for more than 50 percent of total public consumption, its reduction could contribute much to a better fiscal balance and to an improved structure of resource allocation. That is why the economic benefits of the region's peace are so great. Cutting military spending by half would still leave it at more than 10 percent of GNP in Syria, Jordan, and Israel and more than 5 percent in Egypt. But it would release material and human resources—and unmeasurable national energies—for the development and improvement of the living standards of all people in the region. The budgetary savings of such a cut—more than $4.2 billion, or 50 percent of domestic military spending (table 6.6)—would exceed the value of nonmilitary foreign grants to the four countries in 1986. The great gains possible from such a reduction in defense spending could thus dramatically improve the region's economic vitality and prospects.

NOTES

1. ACDA 1988.
2. For a detailed description of sources and estimate methods of military expenditures see Deger 1986, pp. 55-59.
3. While in 1983 the derived domestic military expenditure (DME) in Syria was only $660 million, it increased in 1984 to $2,230 million, a three-fold increase in constant dollars. See ACDA 1987, p. 79 and p. 121. In Egypt too, very wide fluctuations in annual AI/ME and ME/GNP ratios indicate the weakness of the estimates.
4. According to ACDA 1987b, p. 32, there were only 14 nations in 1985 with miltitary spending to GNP ratios of more than 10 percent, 11 of them Middle Eastern countries. The other three were North Korea, Nicaragua, and the Soviet Union.
5. Annual U.S. economic aid to Egypt amounts to $900 million and that of Israel, $1,200 million.
6. If account is given to unofficial information about recent military external loans to Syria and Jordan, this ratio for both might understate the real burden. A distinct advantage of this ratio is the fact that it is net of distortions due to selecting inappropriate conversion factors and exchange rate changes.
7. Bank of Israel 1988, p. 59.
8. In 1985 the total ME/GNP ratio (including AI) was 1.8 percent in Latin America, 4.3 percent in East Asia, and 3.8 percent in Africa (ACDA 1987a, p. 12).
9. World Bank 1989c, table 11.

10. Benoit 1978.
11. Deger 1986, in particular see chapter 8. Chapter 8 embraces a summary of Benoit's major arguments, reference to other works criticizing Benoit's paper, besides Deger's own detailed critique and assessment of Benoit's arguments and findings.
12. Ibid. p.190.
13. Ibid. p. 206.
14. Benoit's results are based on average defense burdens for the years between 1950 and 1965. These values for Egypt, Syria, and Israel were relatively quite low in his study, 6.9 percent, 7.0 percent, and 6.1 percent, respectively. Only for Jordan was the ratio 16.8 percent, the highest values in Benoit's sample. The mean for the 44 countries in the sample was 3.62 percent, and the median was 2.66 percent (Benoit 1978, p. 272).

Table 6.1 Recorded* Military Expenditures
(millions of domestic currency units)

	Syria (LS)		Jordan (JD)		Egypt[a] (LEm)	
	Current prices	Constant 1980 prices[b]	Current prices	Constant 1980 prices[b]	Current prices	Constant 1980 prices[b]
1979	6,190	7,512	114.9	126	772	909
1980	8,804	8,804	118.2	118	1,065	1,065
1981	9,490	8,097	161.2	143	1,475	1,459
1982	10,703	8,994	182.5	153	1,683	1,529
1983	11,309	9,084	196.0	156	2,121	1,781
1984	12,600	9,488	196.8	161	2,385	1,804
1985	13,000	9,123	224.0	177	2,646	1,838
1986	13,600	7,825	249.6	203	2,734	1,683
1987	13,300[d]	5,930[e]	252.8[c]	198	2,986[d]	1,655
1988	14,500[e]	—	256.0[d]	191	3,285[e]	—

* Officially recorded in government budgets. Probably represents domestic military spending only and presumably not full coverage. In Syria and Egypt neither internal security outlays nor capital military outlays are included. Arms imports (AI) and military debt service outlays are not included for any of the three countries.

a. In Egypt from 1980 on, data refer to years starting in July and ending in June of the next calendar year.

b. Deflated by implicit GDP price deflator, based on World Bank 1989e.

c. The very low level of domestic military expenditure (DME) at constant prices in Syria in 1987, is probably biased downward. This bias could be because the overall GDP deflator fails to indicate the actual rise in DME prices in a year in which the GDP deflator has steeply risen by 39 percent. This factor also might overstate to some extent the 14 percent decline in DME in 1986 (a rise of 22 percent of the GDP deflator). Despite these reservations, a deceleration in the growth rate of DME in Syria between 1980 to 1984 is evident, as well as a marked decline in 1985 to 1987 and possibly in 1988 (see tables 6.2 and 6.3 and figure 6.1).

d. Provisional.

e. Budgeted.

Source: National budgetary accounts (cited in IMF and World Bank data).

Table 6.2 Total Defense Spending as a Percentage of GNP, 1954-1986

	1954	*1963*	*1972*	*1979*	*1982*	*1986*
Egypt	6.1	10.0	18.1	11.5	12.6	10.5
Syria	4.2	9.6	15.8	24.7	25.1	22.8
Jordan	20.0	15.8	16.4	14.8	18.2	21.3
All three states	6.4	10.3	17.4	15.7	17.4	15.5
Israel	6.3	10.8	20.8	25.0	25.6	18.2

Source: For the years 1954 to 1979, Sheffer 1984, table 8.3, p. 150. For 1982, own estimates based on table 6.1, adjusted to include arms imports, assuming imports are 40 percent of total military spending. Conversion factors: for Egypt, LE 0.86 = $1 and for Syria LS 4.53 = $1, based on World Bank 1989e. For 1986, see tables 6.5 and 6.1. GNP for Egypt and Syria, World Bank 1988b. Jordan's GNP from IMF data, which includes workers' remittances.

Table 6.3 Military Spending: Annual Real Rates Of Growth, 1954-1987
(percentages)

	1955-1972	1973-1979	1980-1986	1982-1986	1982-1987
Egypt	10.2	0.3	9.2	2.9	2.1
Syria	14.1	18.2	0.6	-0.7[a]	-5.1[a]
Jordan	4.9	11.2	7.1	7.3	5.6
All three states	10.3	6.8	4.8	1.7	-0.9
Israel	15.6	7.5	2.0[b]	-0.4[b]	0.1

a. See note (c) in Table 6.1.
b. Domestic defense consumption, Bank of Israel, various years.
Sources: For 1955-1979, Sheffer 1984, pp. 160-162. For 1980-1987, table 6.1.

Table 6.4 Indices of Military Expenditures, 1954-1984
(Israel = 100)

	1954	1963	1972	1979	1986
Egypt	235	150	90	55	72
Syria	40	35	30	55	90
Jordan	50	20	10	10	24
All three states	320	210	125	120	186
Israel	100	100	100	100	100

Source: For the years 1954-1979, Sheffer 1984, pp. 147, 160-2. For 1986, indices are derived from table 6.5.

Table 6.5 Military Spending: Annual Real Rates of Growth, 1980-1987
(percentages)

	1980	1981	1982	1983	1984	1985	1986	1987[a]
Egypt	17.1	37.0	4.8	16.5	1.3	1.9	-8.4	-1.7
Syria	16.9	-8.0	11.1	1.0	4.4	-3.8	-14.2	-24.2[b]
Jordan	-6.4	20.7	7.1	1.8	3.5	9.9	14.7	-2.5[d]
Israel[c]	14.5	2.0	5.5	1.5	-0.2	-2.5	-5.8	2.2

a. Provisional
b. See note (c) in table 6.1.
c. Domestic defense consumption.
d. Preliminary data indicate a further decline of 3.5 percent in 1988 (table 6.1).
Source: Table 6.1 and Bank of Israel, various years.

Table 6.6 Total Estimated Military Spending, 1986
(converted to $US millions)

	Officially reported (1)	Conversion factor (2)	(1) in $US millions (3)	Estimated military imports[a] ($US millions) (4)	Total (5)
Egypt (LE millions)	42,734	1.30[a]	2,100	1,400	3,500
Syria (LS millions)	13,600	5.21[a]	2,600	1,750	4,350
Jordan (JD millions)	250	0.35[b]	700	470	1,170
Subtotal			**5,440**	**3,650**	**9,020**
Israel (IS billions)	4,715[c]	1.57[b]	3,000	1,840	4,840

a. Conversion factors for Egypt and Syria were calculated as follows: net factor incomes from abroad were added to GDP figures to estimate GNP in domestic currencies, which were divided by GNP in US dollars from World Atlas 1988.
b. Official exchange rates.
c. Domestic public defense consumption.
d. Assuming imports represent 40 percent of total military expenditures. For Israel; actual direct military imports, annual average for the years 1985 to 1987 (Bank of Israel 1988).

Table 6.7 Relative Military Spending
(percentages)

	% of GDP			% of PC		
	Egypt	Syria	Jordan	Egypt	Syria	Jordan
1980	6.5	12.1	12.1	37.5	74.1	48.5
1981	8.5	13.4	13.8	41.2	69.5	56.4
1982	8.1	13.8	13.8	40.4	70.9	56.0
1983	8.8	14.6	13.8	42.8	70.0	56.3
1984	8.4	15.0	13.1	41.8	73.8	52.2
1985	8.0	15.1	13.9	41.7	65.7	55.3
1986	7.1	13.0	15.2	44.0	63.4	54.9
1987*	6.8	10.8[a]	15.0	46.1	62.3	54.4

Note: Reported military spending as percentage of gross domestic product and of public consumption.
a. See note (c) in table 6.1.
* Preliminary.
Source: IMF and World Bank data (see table 6.1).

III
OUTLOOK FOR
REFORM AND
ADJUSTMENT

7

RECOMMENDED POLICY REFORM AND STRUCTURAL CHANGE

The structural, institutional, and policy deficiencies and distortions that undermine economic performance and progress in Egypt, Syria, and Jordan were aggravated by a temporarily favorable external environment and a substantial inflow of foreign aid. Without major reform and sectoral adjustment, these countries probably cannot do what they must to achieve sustained economic growth: diversify their economies and exports and reduce their vulnerability and exposure to external shock. They must attend to long-term adjustment at the same time that they confront deteriorating external circumstances and overcome the current economic crisis. This chapter outlines the structural adjustments and policy reforms these countries must undertake to achieve a more efficient economy and more rational resource allocation.

To substantially raise their income, Egypt, Syria, and Jordan must integrate with the world economy. This means ultimately removing all trade barriers, domestic price controls, and subsidies. To align domestic prices on tradables with international prices, Egypt and Syria must depreciate their currencies and unify them in a single realistic exchange rate. This can be done successfully only with the support of adequate macroeconomic policies. Making these countries' economies more efficient and competitive, with significantly better growth prospects, will require far better public enterprise performance, the adoption of painful policy measures, and structural and institutional changes.

To stimulate diversified exports, the countries must rely more on market forces to determine prices and allocate investments. They must make economic management more effective and use more appropriate government incentives and controls to rationalize economic activities and accelerate export-oriented growth. This does not neccesarily mean that the centrally planned economic regimes of Egypt and Syria must in one stride be turned into capitalistic market economies. But certain reforms and adjustments are needed to rationalize the allocation and use of resources, eliminate unnecessary rigidities and controls, and improve economic performance and productivity.

A key objective should be to increase nontraditional exports. To do this, the three countries must increase exports as a share of GDP, now extremely low. Total non-oil exports of goods amounted in 1988 to less than 4 percent of GDP in Egypt and Syria and 19 percent in Jordan (table 2.6). Improving the prospects for sustained growth means mobilizing domestic resources for investment (to provide extra capacity for exports). So the burden of adjustment falls on consumption—particularly on defense spending, which represents the lion's share of government consumption (table 6.4). Total real domestic consumption must be contained to allow a shift of resources to investments in export activities. The government's role should be to support the development of a technological infrastructure and to design and implement the incentives and reforms needed for export-oriented growth. The government should stop administering prices, exchange rates, or interest rates in a manner that has little relation to market forces.

The Soviet Union and other East European countries are recognizing the need for such a reform program—relying more on market forces and less on centralized administrative controls to determine prices and resource allocation. Reform objectives in these countries are to improve economic performance and the ability to adjust to changing economic conditions, without departing totally from their basic economic ideology.[1] They are contemplating changes in incentive structures, resource allocation, and the government's role in economic life. Reforms aiming to more reliance on market forces are possible in Egypt and Syria without necessarily changing their political and economic regimes.

A healthy balance of payments and domestic stability are crucial for the success of sectoral adjustment aimed at resuming sustainable growth. So a key objective of the first priority should be to restore macroeconomic balance and more appropriate relative prices. Egypt, Syria, and Jordan need to cut fiscal deficits and increase saving to strengthen domestic stability and reduce current account deficits to sustainable levels as a step of utmost importance for economic restructuring. This means, among other things, significantly reducing subsidies and overemployment in the public sector, and devaluing Egyptian and Syrian currencies. The short-term result will be rising commodity prices and unemployment, which especially affect the poor. But the long-term effects of reforming the price structure will be positive. Temporary measures will be needed to relieve the painful transitional effects on the poor of reduced subsidies and public sector employment. Using conditional foreign aid for relief of the poor would remove a key barrier to implementation of recovery programs. Both the World Bank and the International Monetary Fund (IMF) have recently changed their aid policy to make domestic policy reform and structural change a condition for future foreign aid.

As economic conditions in the Third World have worsened, the World Bank's lending strategy to developing countries has changed. Increasingly, the World Bank, while once specialized in project lending, has begun to emphasize loans aimed at improving general economic performance. Previously, developing countries eligible to borrow from the Bank received loans for specific projects that were evaluated and approved in terms of feasibility and reasonable returns on investment. The Bank now recognizes that many such projects, including those with high potential, failed because of the countries' poor economic policies, structural distortions, and weak institutions. Since the early 1980s the Bank's lending has focused more on the broader aspects of the borrower's economy, such as support for policy reform and structural adjustment. The Bank has proportionately increased policy-based lending and economic adjustment loans—and this approach seems more promising.[2] Incentives and loans that encourage more efficient resource allocation, eliminate damaging price and trade controls, and improve domestic and external balances, are likely in the long run to produce higher returns.

The International Monetary Fund (IMF) grants credit under strict conditions. Loans are granted only to member countries with balance of payments problems. The IMF usually insists on domestic demand restraint and exchange rate devaluations geared to quickly reverse balance of payments deficits. There is usually a significant time lag before such policies yield desired results; however, borrowing countries following IMF programs could slide into protracted recession.

The IMF has also recognized the need to design growth-oriented adjustment programs. IMF stabilization programs are often criticized for failing to recognize the need to create new export or import substitution industries. Partly in response to this criticism, the IMF created the Structural Adjustment Facility (SAF) in March 1986. Through adequate financing on concessional terms, this new facility was to promote growth through structural changes in low-income developing countries that faced protracted balance of payments problems. The first SAF loan was to Malawi in July 1988.

Despite basic constraints on long-term development in Egypt, Syria, and Jordan, output could be increased considerably through appropriate incentives, and more efficient government spending and public enterprise operations. Reform should be promoted rapidly to mobilize resources for, and tackle constraints on, growth and development.

Countries outside the Middle East that implement programs to make more efficient use of resources generally carry such efforts out in the framework of stabilization and adjustment programs. Most of these programs emphasize the following:

- More use of market-based pricing than of administrative controls to allocate resources.
- Less of an economic burden on the government and more use of private sector resources.
- More businesslike operation of public enterprises.
- Trade policy that encourages rather than discriminates against exports.

The broad outlines of these reform programs are similar but specific measures must be tailored to the specific needs of each country. Egypt, Syria, and Jordan require reform in three areas: the budget deficit and public spending, incentives, and the public enterprise sector.

THE BUDGET DEFICIT AND PUBLIC SPENDING

An oversize budget deficit—more than 20 percent of GDP in Egypt, Syria, and Jordan—is the root cause of many macroeconomic problems. Large deficits create excess demand for imports and fuel domestic inflation. Much of the balance of payments deficit can be traced to budget imbalances—the direct result of heavy imports for subsidized consumption and the public investment program, and the indirect result of fiscal expansion, which causes aggregate demand to exceed domestic supply. The two top-priority policy changes to improve the balance of payments in these three countries would be to substantially reduce the budget deficit and stop relying on bank loans.

All three countries must reduce public spending, which is at an unsustainable level. As soon as possible, they must (a) substantially cut direct subsidies on food products,[3] (b) increase selected industrial prices to correct distortions and improve the financial performance of public sector companies, and (c) increase energy prices to eliminate the gap between current prices and the alternative cost of energy.[4] Implementing these policies means dropping subsidies on inessential items, targeting the remaining subsidies to low-income groups, and raising the prices of subsidized commodities over time. None of these measures is easy to administer, but they are essential if the budget is to be adjusted.

In addition, Egypt and Syria must reduce public sector responsibilities and employment, which have become unmanageably large. In both countries it is government policy to use the public sector as employer of last resort. So, for instance, between 1980 and 1985 public sector employment grew 6.5 percent a year in Egypt, providing nearly half of all new jobs. But the private sector should be the source of new job opportunities. In the long run public sector reform should reduce the government's employment and wage bill and make the public sector more efficient and productive. This in turn will increase the average public sector wage, attracting abler employees to government service.

The budget deficit should also be reduced by raising tax revenues. The consumption tax and customs duties are important budget items in Egypt, Syria, and Jordan. But certain taxes distort resource allocation. The personal income tax in these countries produced proportionately less revenue than in the developing world. As part of tax reform, the tax base should be broadened to include more items, and some items should be taxed ad valorem—all commodities liable for import duty, for example. Linking government revenues to national expenditures will make the budgets more flexible. Also, taxing commodities without discrimination at the source of production will prevent distortion of production incentives.

The above measures will help increase revenues, reduce subsidies, and contain growth in expenditures. But lowering the deficit to an average below 5 percent of GDP will no doubt require big cuts in public investment and military spending. The public investment programs in these countries are currently large (17 to 18 percent of GDP in Egypt,[5] 14 percent in Syria,[6] and 20 percent in Jordan[7]). The real level of public investment can be reduced to less than 10 percent of GDP and still provide everything essential for the reform program. So large a reduction is possible because a lot is spent on low-return projects and programs, substantial investments have already been made in infrastructure, and several large projects—especially in steel, cement, and fertilizers—are near completion. As public investments shrink there should be a change in priorities and a larger role for the private sector. Priority should be given to maintenance and rehabilitation, particularly on transport, urban infrastructure, and public utility projects. Enough investment priority should be given to export-oriented industries to change the structure of the economy. And the cuts in military and domestic spending that the three governments started in recent years (table 6.3 and figure 6.1), as economic conditions deteriorated, should be continued to support macroeconomic balance and structural adjustment.

INCENTIVES

Syria, Egypt, and Jordan are small economies that must significantly increase diversified exports as a share of GDP. This requires strategic policies on exchange rates and agricultural prices (for both food and commodity exports). Exchange rates have been overvalued in all three countries for too much and too long. Exports of agricultural and manufactured commodities have stagnated and been unable to keep pace with rising imports. In the 1970s, the internal terms of trade shifted against agriculture, especially for export crops. The growing demand for foreign exchange was at first met by the surge of foreign aid and loans, and then by resorting to import licensing and exchange control. Thus by the early 1980s Egypt and Syria had active illegal markets in foreign exchange and bartered goods. Devaluation of domestic currencies—an increasingly pressing need—will help reduce the balance of payments deficits and shift the internal terms of trade in favor of those who produce for export and away from those who consume imports. The Syrian and Egyptian currencies have been partly devalued, but the system of multiple exchange rates must still be corrected. This means getting the exchange rate closer to the equilibrium rate through further devaluations and unification of all foreign exchange transactions. At the margin this unification will improve incentives for nonpetroleum exports, tourism, and workers' remittances. Reform of the exchange rate should obviate the need for administrative restrictions on imports, making a more efficient economic policy possible.

Changes of this type that have recently begun in Egypt include substitution of the import licensing system by a system of different categories of goods with different tariff rates. This move is important for long-term economic adjustment and a more efficient structure for domestic production. But fear of the social and political consequences of exchange rate reform may delay or minimize exchange rate adjustment. Such resistance originates among those people—often the urban middle class—who benefit from the implicit subsidies of overvalued currency. But the distributional effects of devaluation, which differ with different economic structures, are most likely to benefit middle income groups in Egypt, Syria, and Jordan. Moreover, devaluation allows for the removal of controls and trade restrictions that create artificial scarcities. In the short run, it is true that the poor may be harmed by the higher prices of basic consumption goods that will result, so measures must be contemplated to relieve the hardship of the poor.

The import control system in Egypt, Syria, and Jordan protects domestic production at highly variable rates. Imports of some items are altogether banned, while others have tariffs that are either very high (final products) or very low (intermediate and capital goods and raw materials). The result is that some products are produced at very high (domestic resource) cost, with little prospect for export. Trade policy reform must create the right incentives for domestic producers to export goods. Quotas and other quantitative controls should be banned and the tariff structure should be as simple and uniform as possible. Taxation of luxury goods should be implemented by a tax on the consumption of those goods, not their importation. Taxing their importation encourages inefficient domestic production.

Implementing trade reform too speedily in Egypt, Syria, and Jordan may be a problem given their complex systems of import control systems and incentives for different producers. A gradual approach would allow domestic producers to adjust to world market conditions without greatly disrupting production. Reducing and eliminating tariff differentials among different import categories calls for painful adjustment by domestic firms. Foreign aid flows and a gradual approach to adjustment may ease the private and social cost of reform.

A major aim of policy reform should be to change the distorted system of incentives in the agricultural sector. This incentive structure is inadequate for both producers and consumers. In Syria, for example, domestic procurement prices for the major internationally traded crops (except cotton) are higher than international prices. The government established these prices to encourage farmers to expand output. But with world prices declining, domestic prices of crops such as wheat, maize, and sugarbeets are now so high that they encourage marginal producers, give relatively efficient producers excessive rents, and divert resources for production of other profitable but unsupported crops. Moreover, because of the government's long-term commitment to maintaining low prices on basic foodstuffs, these high output prices have resulted in huge subsidies to food processing and distribution. At a time when farmers were officially being paid an average SL 1,230 a ton for wheat, and the government was importing flour at about SL 1,070 a ton, flour was being sold domestically at SL 142.5 a ton to state bakeries for the production of low-priced bread. Similarly, the retail price for a monthly allotment of sugar is less than one third the raw material cost of sugarbeets.

Attention to inefficiencies in the agricultural sector should be an important part of policy reform and adjustment for both Egypt and Syria. Because of the sector's relative flexibility (in terms of crop composition), high employment, and low foreign exchange needs, its role is especially important in a period of austerity and balance of payments difficulties. Despite severe land constraints, agricultural production could be increased considerably, restoring it to a respectable long-term growth trend. Promotion of local food production is crucial to slowing the tide of increasing agricultural imports. Controls on area and input should be relaxed as they constrain farmers' ability to respond to economic incentives.[8] Efforts should also be directed at liberalizing input distribution, strengthening research and extension, upgrading water distribution and drainage, and streamlining coordinating institutional arrangements among the ministries that design and implement agricultural policy.

Reform of incentives also means adjusting domestic interest rates. Commercial bank interest rates in Egypt, Syria, and Jordan are too low and poorly designed. The narrow spread between short- and long-term deposit rates provides little incentive to save and the rates are not positive in real terms. Egyptians, for example, have the option of holding financial assets in foreign currencies that currently earn 7 to 8 percent (in U.S. dollars). Given low deposit rates on the pound, their narrow spread, and expected depreciation of the pound/dollar exchange rate, there is virtually no incentive for Egyptians to hold financial assets in pound accounts.[9] Thus, Egyptian monetary policy should encourage more voluntary conversion of foreign currency into domestic assets. This would require pound deposit rates at least 5 to 6 percent above the rate of inflation. Such an adjustment would decrease the growth of liquidity and increase the availability of foreign exchange for domestic production.

Because of low savings, all three countries need foreign capital to build up their capital stock. All of them have run into foreign debt troubles because of borrowing too much in the past—and their investments have not been productive enough to generate the foreign currency earnings needed to service those debts in the future. They have often invested foreign loans in low-return projects and public consumption.

Not enough is done to encourage domestic savings instead of borrowing abroad. To do so, they must develop domestic financial markets. Governments tend to distort domestic financial systems, by forcing intermediaries to lend at low or negative interest rates in real terms with the aim of stimulating investments. But artificially low interest rates stimulate surplus demand for funds. Then allocation of credit must be administered. Instead, interest rates should be allowed to rise and clear the market so more deposits are available to fund more investments and so loans need not be "directed." In other words, reform of the financial market would stimulate both domestic savings and investments. Savers would get a real return for their deposits and borrowers would not invest in wrong projects, which distorted interest rates make possible. Real interest rates have been artificially low (indeed, negative) because administered rates have not kept up with inflation.[10] Governments should stop putting rigid ceilings on interest rates and avoid putting pressure on banks to favor certain borrowers. They should establish the legal framework in which financial markets can develop—so lenders and borrowers can meet. And they should encourage the growth of security markets and other financial intermediaries to supply longer-term loans. A realistic interest rates policy could promote the development of efficient capital markets.

These governments have financed part of their deficits by borrowing in domestic markets, forcing banks to lend to them at low interest rates. This obviously limits the banks' ability to lend to the private sector. Sound public finance is critical to the development of more efficient domestic financial markets for private borrowers.

RATIONALIZING THE PUBLIC SECTOR

The state plays a larger role in the economies of Egypt and Syria—and to a lesser degree Jordan—than in most other countries. There are proportionately more public enterprises in these countries than in most other developing countries, and they engage in more kinds of activities. Public investment accounts for 70 percent of investments in Egypt and 60 percent in Syria.[11] The rapid growth, inefficient management, and overambitious public investment programs of the public sector, are important factors in the economic difficulties facing Egypt, Syria, and Jordan (chapter 3). The scope of public sector activities and the operating subsidies to which public enterprises have access stifle private activity in agriculture, industry, and commerce.

The public sector in all three countries suffers from the same interrelated problems: poor management that lacks autonomy, distorted pricing, poor financial performance, outmoded technology, labor problems, and most recently, inadequate access to imports. The key element of reform should be to ensure price flexibility. This is essential for correcting the distorted incentive system created by price controls and for allowing efficient managers to achieve their targets without financial constraints. Second, reform should ensure managers autonomy in hiring, firing, wages and other incentives, and in investment decisions. Third, reform should provide financial self-reliance by eliminating government assistance. Finally, the governments of all three countries should consider privatizing many enterprises whose public stature was fortified in the past by a national strategic interest. For example, the metal industry in Egypt and the cement industry in Jordan already include private firms, on a small scale. This process should be encouraged by privatizing public firms in these and other industries.

NOTES

1. Since these lines were written, dramatic political changes have taken place in Eastern Europe. It appears that people in these countries want to replace their centralized economic systems with market-oriented economies of the western model. It is still too early to assess the ultimate outcome of these revolutionary developments.

2. World Bank 1988a, p. 65.

3. In Egypt the total subsidy bill in the fiscal 1988 budget amounted to 5.3 percent of GDP and a much larger percentage if implicit subsidies are included. World Bank 1989b, p. 130.

4. Even after increasing energy prices in Egypt in recent years, the weighted average of domestic petroleum prices (after the most recent increase in March 1989) did not exceed 36 percent of world prices, and electricity tariffs 24 percent of the long-run marginal cost. Ibid, p. 130.

5. Egypt, Ministry of Planning (IMF 1988, p. 54).

6. Syria, Central Bureau of Statistics (IMF 1989, p. 66).

7. World Bank, 1989b, p. 227.

8. Substantial progress has been made recently in Egypt in adjusting agricultural sector policies. Crop area allotments and delivery quotas at low prices were eliminated for all crops except cotton, sugar cane, and half of the rice crop. Ibid., p. 131. It should however be emphasized that cotton and rice are the most important field crops in Egypt.

9. Rates on deposits under six months maturity, which account for the bulk of domestic currency deposits, were not changed in the May 1989 reform and at present range from 5.0 percent to 8.5 percent, much below the rate of inflation of 25 percent in fiscal 1988 and 20 percent in fiscal 1989.

10. Low or negative real interest rates on loans had over the years induced capital-intensive projects at the expense of employment.

11. These shares declined in recent years in both countries due to budgetary constraints and policies to encourage private investors. In the early 1980s the proportion of public investments reached 80 to 90 percent (IMF 1988 and 1989).

8

PROMOTING SUSTAINED GROWTH WITH FOREIGN AID

For foreign aid to promote sustained growth it is important that it be granted in the right way and in reasonable amounts. Foreign aid could help Egypt, Syria, and Jordan restructure their economies and strengthen inadequate institutions and economic policies. But to be effective foreign aid should be spread over ten years, to allow time to implement the reforms and adjustments needed for more efficient economic performance. Foreign aid could support efforts to expand exports and strengthen the balance of payments. The ultimate objective should be to gradually reduce the recipient countries' dependence on foreign aid.

Foreign aid can be provided in several ways: as support for specific projects, including regional joint development programs; as grants of general assistance to bolster the balance of payments; and as conditional assistance aimed at encouraging adequate policy measures and structural adjustment to improve the economic environment and the use of resources. For the economies under review—heavily burdened with foreign debt—all foreign aid should be provided as grants rather than loans.

Experience suggests that unconditional foreign aid, even if linked to specific projects, is likely to delay rather than promote painful reforms. Foreign aid should not be used to perpetuate inefficient structures and economic policies. When the economic environment and economic performance are poor, external aid will fail to sustain growth and support progress toward economic independence.

Drastic change is essential in the economic policies and resource allocation of Egypt, Syria, and Jordan. And policy reform and structural adjustment—prerequisites for economic growth—are likely to yield relatively high economic returns. The governments of these three states are well aware of the weaknesses of their economies, but are often reluctant to take corrective steps because of short-run effects on the poorer classes. Realignment of prices and cuts in public spending are not popular, and even administrations that are inclined to relax controls do not hasten to do so. So conditional foreign aid can be crucial to reform and by providing transitional assistance to the poor can ameliorate a major obstacle to change.

Supporters of a Special Development Fund for the Middle East sometimes claim that foreign aid can foster both economic growth and peace by focusing on the development of cross-country joint projects and regional economic cooperation. It is presumed that economic cooperation could stabilize and safeguard peace between Israel and its neighboring countries—once a peace settlement is agreed upon—through increasing interdependence and creating vested interests in peace.[1] From an economic point of view, this is probably not the best way to use limited resources. Not that regional cooperation on joint projects would not benefit the parties concerned—but the list of feasible joint projects with high economic returns is short. And the record of developing countries worldwide is not studded with successes in regional economic cooperation. It would not be a good idea to impose economic cooperation on Egypt, Syria, Jordan, and Israel through the lure of additional external aid. Providing direct foreign aid to each country through a development fund seems the more promising way to promote sustained economic growth in the region, provided it is aimed at improving economic performance or export diversification. Of course, some regional projects—such as the development of tourism facilities—could produce high economic returns provided all parties concerned agree to cooperate without external pressure.

SUPPORT FOR ECONOMIC REFORM

The objective of policy support is to improve both economic performance and the allocation and use of resources. In Egypt, Syria, and Jordan it is crucial (in different degrees of urgency) to remove price controls and subsidies and adjust exchange rates. Corrective price measures will have short-term adverse effects on the social conditions of the urban poor, however—and in Egypt, Syria, and Jordan more than half of the population lives in urban areas. So political and social considerations are major obstacles to devaluation and the removal of subsidies and administrative price controls. Foreign aid should be designed to support these reforms. Foreign aid should be sizable enough to provide both immediate and continuing support. Only then will recipient governments have the confidence to sustain reform programs. And support should be dependent on the maintenance of reforms.

It is crucial to reduce budgetary spending, particularly on subsidies and defense, and eliminate fiscal deficits and wasteful public activities. Short-sighted politicians generally avoid such unpopular measures, which often bring about a short-term rise in unemployment. But a temporary rise in unemployment is the cost of achieving a better macroeconomic balance and structural changes that favor the traded sectors.

Stabilization measures will reduce final domestic uses, including imports. They will also stimulate the growth of exports, provided their impact is not eroded by overvalued currencies. In the short run, declining imports will be the main way to reduce the current account deficit to tolerable levels. In the longer run, improving the external balance of payments will require export expansion, since imports are bound to grow as the economy grows. Any reform program must also take into account the heavy external debt burdens of these countries, in particular Egypt's (see chapter 2). Rapidly increasing exports will help reduce the debt servicing ratio to more tolerable dimensions. This is a formidable task, but the key to growth and economic transformation. A weak balance of payments may jeopardize policy reform and undermine sustained growth. So incremental foreign aid should focus on supporting policies aimed at improving the balance of payments. This initially requires appropriate macroeconomic policies and the adjustment of relative prices, in particular key prices such as the exchange rate. Another important component of any comprehensive recovery program is a long-term rescheduling scheme for foreign debts, because debt servicing is an excessive financial burden for the three countries.

Foreign aid is counterproductive if it weakens the resolve of governments to tackle developmental problems. Aid is no substitute for domestic programs that create incentives and the institutions needed to increase domestic production. So foreign aid to Egypt, Syria, and Jordan should be conditional. Donors and governments should establish and agree upon quantitative, well-defined targets for removing price controls and subsidies, reducing fiscal deficits, and unifying multiple exchange rates at realistic levels. During the difficult transitional period of stabilization efforts and price adjustments, extra foreign aid may be needed to alleviate the burden on the poor and induce governments to proceed with painful reforms. Policy reform is a long, politically difficult process. It requires much time and patience until the benefits of the program are apparent. Unless donors sustain their support, any reforms may be short-lived. At the same time, foreign aid is by its nature temporary and should be allocated in such a way that the recipient countries move toward economic independence.

SUPPORT FOR BASIC PROGRAMS

Major economic policy reform in Egypt, Syria, and Jordan is likely over time to bring about sectoral restructuring. An improved macroeconomic environment and adjustments in relative prices will encourage a better reallocation of productive factors. Abolishing price distortions and restoring fiscal balance are crucial for efficient use of resources and good economic performance. But the three countries face basic constraints on development: escalating population growth, low levels of education and training, and health problems that undermine physical and intellectual development—not to mention technological backwardness in agriculture and industry. Programs to address these issues have been initiated but are threatened by the declining trend in per capita incomes, foreign currency receipts, and widespread crisis and stagnation. The shortage of resources for such programs is likely to continue for several years. Foreign aid programs are urgently needed to address these long-term constraints on a sustainable basis.

Aid donors should work with the governments to develop realistic programs. In general, socioeconomic programs should be designed and implemented to be low-cost, well-targeted, and replicable. A funding program is of central importance in formulating efficient sectoral strategies. The program should be designed to achieve program objectives, rather than be constrained by lending or granting procedures. Donor assistance should strike a balance between adequate funding of recurrent expenditures (operations and maintenance on ongoing activities) and support for new projects and new physical capacity.

Recipient governments and donors must both commit themselves to providing long-term support for socioeconomic programs. These programs should not be the residual legatees of domestic funds. And aid agencies should treat support to the social sector as basic to assistance. External support should be continuous and reliable, provided that agreed-upon policy measures are being implemented. Without commitments from both recipient governments and donors, the basic impediments to economic growth and the alleviation of poverty—poor health and low levels of education and skills—will remain.

Efficient capital markets must exist if economic performance is to improve. Capital markets facilitate privatization and structural adjustments and promote economic growth. In Egypt and Syria the government absorbs most available savings, using them to finance budgetary and other public sector requirements. This has also been the case in Israel, where capital markets were for a long time almost entirely "nationalized." Only recently has capital market reform been introduced in Israel with the aim of limiting the government's role and opening the market gradually to the business sector. Governments in all four countries should provide the facilities needed to strengthen and develop financial institutions that mobilize funds for investors. The strengthening of stock exchanges and other financial institutions should also be supported. A realistic interest rate policy is, as already noted above,[2] a key element in the creation of efficient capital markets. The development of financial markets deserves more attention than it now gets as a key to mobilizing additional resources for development and economic restructuring.

It takes time to bring about sectoral adjustment and strengthen institutions, and benefits are not immediately apparent. Increasing nontraditional exports as a share of GDP may take years. During the transitional period, foreign aid should be used primarily to promote basic adjustment programs. Without major structural and institutional adjustment, the prospects for sustained growth and eventual independence from foreign aid are grim. Egypt, Syria, and Jordan must mobilize more domestic resources and allocate them more productively to solve current difficulties and promote growth. The role of foreign aid should be to induce and support efforts to make these three economies more productive and competitive. This kind of external involvement in the support of policy reform and structural adjustment should not be interpreted as infringing on the sovereignty of the recipient states. External aid should be conditional on economic adjustment programs that the countries have fully accepted.

DEBT RESCHEDULING

Debt servicing difficulties reflect the underlying economic weakness, particularly the inefficient use of investment, in Egypt, Syria, and Jordan. Attempts to improve economic performance will be frustrated unless these countries are relieved of some of their immediate debt-service obligations.[3] The debt-service problem has been aggravated by the current declining trend in foreign currency receipts and in per capita income in all three countries. The basic economic need is to raise real per capita income, but reversing this downward trend will take several years.

Much of the debt service—including the servicing of loans from the World Bank and other preferred multilateral creditors, and previously rescheduled debt—is ineligible for rescheduling. Moreover, trade credit and arrears of trade credit represent a significant part of the debt servicing burden.[4] Payment of these obligations is critical for maintaining trade, and the interest component is ineligible for rescheduling. The wide range of unreschedulable obligations that Egypt, Syria, and Jordan face means that the immediate burden of repayment accounts for a significant proportion of the total debt-service obligations.

Donors should be flexible in assessing these countries' debt servicing problems especially during policy reform and major structural adjustment. Debt relief can be used to support reform programs, because it releases foreign exchange that can immediately be used for imports. Debt relief is most valuable when continued over several years, however. Multiyear debt relief and longer grace periods should be part of any package of financial support for monitorable reform programs.

A SPECIAL DEVELOPMENT FUND (SDF)

In recent years various political personalities have proposed establishing a Special Development Fund for the Middle East in the belief that such a Fund could foster peace through economic development and regional economic cooperation. Such a Fund, were it to materialize, should focus on supporting the reforms and adjustments most likely to help resolve prevailing economic difficulties and create the right environment for economic progress. The SDF could be financed by the rich Arab oil countries and the Western industrialized countries (especially the United States) that have a special interest in promoting a lasting peace in the Middle East. The key to the Fund's success would be enough resources to allow for long-term commitments of economic aid. Grants should be conditional to ensure the promotion of sustained growth and eventual independence from foreign aid.

We have emphasized that external assistance, by itself, is not the solution for the troubled economies of the Middle East. Better use of internal and external resources must be the focus of attention. Without major changes in economic programs and policies, no amount of external assistance can bring about a lasting increase in per capita income. Unless aid recipients implement policy reform and structural adjustment, foreign aid will only increase consumption—temporarily.

Each government should agree to the conditions and components of the program (and pace of implementation) for which aid is given. A long time is needed for structural and institutional adjustments, so aid should be spread over ten years, in several stages. Grants should be given in semi-annual installments, conditional on progress in implementing policy reform and economic adjustments.

The first stage of the adjustment program—stabilization and price reforms—should take three to four years. Establishing quantitative progress targets for this stage should be relatively easy. Annual targets for reducing fiscal deficits until their final elimination, for example, are achievable in the first stage. Specific annual targets for reducing defense spending, subsidies, and other unnecessary public expenditures should also be considered. A target date for unifying multiple exchange rates in a single realistic exchange rate and for trade liberalization is also feasible during this first stage. Gradual targets for removal of price controls and import restrictions could be agreed upon and quantitative targets for tax and other policy reforms could be defined.

Targets should not be too ambitious and each state should agree on the quantitative performance criteria to be used to measure progress in economic policy reform. Highest priority in the first stage should be given to removing price distortions and all import and other damaging administrative controls, and to restoring a fiscal balance and monetary restraint that support price and trade liberalization. Stabilization and the alignment of relative prices should improve economic performance and facilitate structural adjustment. The amount of foreign aid should be large in the early years of adjustment so that balance of payments difficulties would not jeopardize the implementation of reforms. Later on, SDF support could gradually be reduced, tapering to nothing after 10 years.

Performance criteria for measuring progress in structural adjustment would be set at the end of stage one. That would be the time to identify weak institutions that should be strengthened and state-owned enterprises that should be sold or restructured. That would also be the time to agree upon ways to make management of public sector enterprises more efficient. Support for these and other basic adjustments should begin when the Fund's operations are initiated, and progress checkups scheduled for individual projects should be designed in stage two.

Growth must be oriented towards exports, with highest priority given to supporting development of needed infrastructure and facilities that promote the expansion of exports. Government should usually refrain from direct involvement in the establishment of export plants, because governments are influenced by noneconomic considerations. Government's role should be to create favorable conditions for export activities—for example, by restoring appropriate exchange rates, giving exporters access to credit, developing adequate facilities for export credit insurance, promoting overseas marketing, and providing facilities to help small and new exporters. By restoring macroeconomic balance, removing controls and price distortions, and interfering less in management of the economy, the government will make the economy more efficient and competitive, and that will promote exports. The rise in private sector exports in Syria and Egypt in 1986-1987, appeared to be a strong response to favorable changes in relative prices and other domestic conditions. Manufacturers' exports increased in Syria from $270 million in 1985 to $440 million in 1987 and in Egypt from $640 million to $1,020 million.[5] These developments at least should weaken opposition by authorities in these countries to adjustments in exchange rates on grounds of ineffectiveness and the inelasticity of exports to exchange rates changes.

The SDF should also grant aid to modernize vocational training and other facilities that would increase productivity. The Fund could support such approved projects as the expansion and equipment of technical schools, higher level training facilities for technicians, and the promotion of computerization and modern communication systems. The proposed Fund's share of aid allocations to support basic economic adjustment should greatly increase after major policy reforms are completed. Aid to encourage privatization should be considered, particularly for Egypt and Syria, where privatization would contribute greatly to efficiency and sectoral restructuring.

The success of a reform program depends on the government's determination to carry out needed reforms and adjustments. SDF should grant aid that supports sound policies in countries which take the steps needed to stabilize and restructure their economies in order to secure sustained growth and achieve economic independence.

SDF aid must be based on a well-designed, growth-oriented, long-term program that allows for a time lag between policy and adjustment measures and their results and benefits. Such a program would differ from existing bilateral and multilateral aid programs in both character and conditionality. Other programs are less comprehensive, cover a shorter time span, and focus less on creating export-oriented growth. The SDF should also work more harmoniously with recipient governments.

In the past the United States, the USSR, and the rich Arab oil states poured substantial aid into Egypt, Syria, Jordan, and Israel (table 1.1). Most of that aid was spent on armaments or on public and private consumption, and contributed little to a permanent solution to basic economic problems. The SDF would support measures to increase efficiency and productivity and to mitigate long-term constraints on growth. The SDF should support measures to improve economic performance rather than to build engineering projects in an inefficient economic environment. The SDF programs should provide hope for a better future to the peoples of the Middle East.

The economic distress of the Palestinian refugees and the people of devastated Lebanon could also be alleviated through special development programs. These are beyond the scope of our study, but economic expansion in Egypt, Syria, Jordan, and Israel—and the promotion of normal economic relations among them—would greatly improve the economic conditions of the Palestinians and the Lebanese.

NOTES

1. See Shahar, Fishelson and Hirch 1989, chapter 1.
2. See chapter 7.
3. See chapter 2 and table 2.7.
4. Amortization of suppliers' credits reached $1.5 billion in 1988 in Egypt (Central Bank of Egypt).
5. World Bank 1989e.

9

EXTERNAL RESOURCE FLOWS

Earlier chapters emphasized that a flow of external resources cannot guarantee development and sustained growth. Without appropriate policies, no amount of external assistance can reverse the recent economic decline in the Middle East. And yet policy reform to promote growth will be unsustainable without additional resources. A long-term estimate of a country's resource requirements is always difficult. The problem in Egypt, Syria, and Jordan is worse than usual, because massive shifts are needed in relative prices and in the pattern of resource use—and these shifts may overturn the historical relationship on which calculations might be based. Projections for oil prices, military spending, exchange rates, and workers' remittances are all uncertain. Nor is it possible to say whether Egypt, Jordan, and Syria will develop credible policy reform and thus be eligible for additional aid from international organizations.

Despite these uncertainties, we try in this chapter to estimate the magnitude of aid requirements of these three economies in the 1990s. The objective embodied in these estimates is to reverse the decline in per capita income and achieve in the forthcoming decade moderate but sustainable growth rates of 2 to 3 percent a year in per capita GDP in the 1990s. All three countries have rapidly growing populations, so this objective can be achieved only if the GDP growth rate reaches at least 6 percent a year. Our estimate of external resource requirements for the 1990s is based on minimum estimated imports needed to achieve investment levels consistent with 6-percent GDP growth, in the light of maximum feasible exports and domestic savings feasible in the first half of the 1990s. These estimates are not econometric projections based on historical trends and relationships (as in Lavy 1984), but on modified current structures and policies for new growth patterns.

We estimate the minimum flow of foreign exchange needed to pay for imports and debt servicing, after allowing for a reasonable increase in export earnings and continued favorable debt relief. One can estimate the foreign exchange requirements based either on import requirements or on investment requirements. It is all the same whether external resource needs are calculated as the gap between import needs and export capacity or as the gap between investment and domestic savings, for the two are identical.

Even if great efforts are made to diversify and expand exports and even if foreign debt is generously rescheduled, a substantial foreign exchange gap is likely to persist until 1995. This gap might reach $8 billion annually in Egypt (including $5.6 billion debt servicing), $1 billion in Syria, and $800 million in Jordan. If debt-relief facilities are larger, the financing gaps would be smaller. Prospects for bridging these gaps with foreign exchange from abroad are not bright. Domestic savings must be increased more than is necessary to support essential investments, if these countries are to implement the reforms needed to improve economic performance, competitiveness, and efficiency in the use of domestic resources. Otherwise, it seems doubtful that the per capita growth target of 2 to 3 percent could be achieved—without a jump in oil prices and external aid. A surge in the savings ratio, particularly in the public sector, is crucial to growth.

FOREIGN EXCHANGE REQUIREMENTS

The Import Gap

Import capacity is inadequate for implementing adjustment and growth programs in Egypt, Syria, and Jordan. Real per capita imports have been declining recently, especially in Syria. To finance growth-oriented adjustment and to support sustained, rapid growth in total output and per capita consumption, this trend should be reversed. Imports in the 1990s should grow faster than GDP growth. At a minimum, real per capita imports are likely to return to levels achieved during recent episodes of fast output growth. With restructuring of the economy and renewed growth, domestic production may replace imports, but only in the medium or longer run. During 1983-1985 the Egyptian economy grew an average 7 percent a year, and the import-to-GDP ratio was 0.35. In the following two years the growth rate fell to 2.5 percent a year and imports as a share of GDP declined to 0.25. In previous episodes of fast economic growth, Egypt's import-to-GDP ratio also ranged from 0.35 to 0.40. This range is typical for more developed economies that experience fast growth, such as South Korea in the last two decades (0.35-0.40), Côte d'Ivoire in the 1970s (0.45-0.50), Tunisia in the 1980s (0.5), and Turkey in recent years (0.30). With inadequate imports of basic raw materials and inputs, production is greatly constrained, and the scope for import substitution is limited. To renew growth in the Egyptian economy, import ratios must reach their former high levels. To recover that import ratio, given projected GDP growth of 6 percent and higher import prices, Egypt's annual import requirements for several years may be $19 to $20 billion in current prices (compared with $17 billion in 1985).

The pattern of imports is similar in Syria: output growth fell sharply as imports fell. During 1979-1982 output grew an average 7 percent a year, and the import-to-GDP ratio was 0.36. In the most recent recession (1984-1987) the import ratio fell to 0.17. Syria's level of imports, especially non-oil imports, has been determined by the availability of foreign exchange. Acute foreign exchange shortages since 1983 have led to a decline in imports and raw materials for such sectors as metal and metal products, machinery, transport, and other equipment. The level of non-oil merchandise imports (imported mostly by the public sector) fell from $2,660 million in 1983 to $1,640 million in 1988 (table 2.6). Oil imports also fell sharply. In 1986 Syria became a net oil exporter, largely as a result of increased domestic production and import requirements that fell as the economy contracted. If the economy is to return to a path of sustained growth, non-oil imports will have to rise in line with economic expansion to levels achieved in the early 1980s. Assuming higher import prices and faster economic growth, a conservative estimate of non-oil imports of goods and services means foreign exchange requirements averaging $4.5 to 5 billion a year for the next five years (compared with $3,892 million in 1983 and $3,171 million in 1987).[1]

In Jordan before the early 1980s, sustained high external receipts sustained a high level of imports. At their peak in 1982, total merchandise import payments exceeding $3.2 billion were six times higher than receipts from domestic exports. In subsequent years, the value of imports declined because of a slowdown in domestic demand, government policy initiatives designed to encourage import substitution (including a gradual real depreciation of the dinar), and a decline in international prices for crude oil and other commodities. The value of imports declined 23 percent between 1983 and 1987, and by 1987 was 27 percent below the peak level of 1982.[2]

Estimating Jordan's future import needs is difficult. The nominal value of imports increased only by 2 percent in 1988, reflecting a small real decline. The import-to-GDP ratio, however, was relatively stable during this period. Using the same approach we used for Egypt and Syria, we estimate Jordan's import requirements for goods and services to be $5 billion a year (similar to 1983, table 9.1).

Debt Servicing

Between 1990 and 1995, scheduled debt service payments—including payments to international organizations and the Soviet Union—are projected to rise to about $5.6 billion a year in Egypt, $540 million in Syria (excluding military debt service to the Soviet Union), and $1 billion in Jordan, against actual payments (in 1987) of $1,734 million, $365 million, and $734 million, respectively. The situation is particularly serious in Egypt and Jordan. These Middle Eastern countries cannot escape economic crisis without a sizable reduction in their debt burden.[3]

Egypt's foreign debt payment obligations (interest and amortization) jumped from $3.2 billion in 1983 to $4.8 billion in 1986 (table 2.7), excluding military debt, and declined to $2.5 billion in 1988 due to rescheduling. Unable to service its debt, Egypt had accumulated arrears of $6.9 billion by 1987, which were rescheduled by the Paris club that year. Ignoring future financing needs, the debt stock at the end of 1988 would require debt service payments of almost $5.6 billion a year until 1992, if no further debt relief arrangements are agreed upon.

The severity of Jordan's debt burden was revealed only recently. Outstanding medium- and long-term external debt at the end of 1988 amounted to $8 billion, 160 percent of Jordan's GNP. In 1987 scheduled debt service payments amounted to just over half a billion dollars, against an underestimated $3.7 billion in debt. The debt service burden is expected to be close to $1 billion a year in the first half of the 1990s unless major rescheduling is arranged.

Syria's external debt obligation seems on the surface to be less disturbing but information is scarce on the terms and structure of Syria's external debt, on arrears, and on military debt.[4] The official estimated medium- and long-term civilian debt was $2.8 billion at the end of 1988, up from $2.7 the previous year. World Bank data show Syrian debt in 1988 at $3.7 billion, of which roughly $600 million was arrears. Total outstanding arrears were estimated at $800 million at the end of 1988, $168 million of it owed to the World Bank. Syria's average annual debt service payment for 1990-1995 is an estimated $500 million, excluding payments to the Soviet Union on military debt.

Export Earnings

In the long run, export earnings should be the principal source of financing for external payments. These earnings must finance both growing import requirements and debt servicing. All three countries have been exporting mainly oil and labor services, neither of which can grow much in the near future. Adjustment policies should help shift resources to export activities, increase manufactured and agricultural exports, and thus diversify the sources of foreign exchange earnings. Except for textiles, manufactured exports are at particularly low levels: only $330 million in Egypt in 1987, $165 million in Syria in 1987; and $380 million in Jordan (excluding mineral exports).

Egypt has shown signs of rising non-oil merchandise exports since 1986, after more than a decade of stagnation. In response to a severe balance of payments crisis, trade policy was liberalized, and foreign exchange rate and other pricing policies were reformed. These changes, together with depressed domestic demand, have stimulated non-oil exports. Further improvement will require more adjustment measures aimed at removing rigidities and improving efficiency, and thus helping to redirect underused capacity and new resources to exports.

Egypt's major export earnings are from workers' remittances and oil exports. Unless real international oil prices rise significantly before the mid-1990s, earnings from oil exports are unlikely to increase rapidly. Egyptian workers abroad do not transfer all their savings home, however, so Egypt could attract more of these savings by offering higher exchange and interest rates and by liberalizing the domestic economy. If domestic energy prices continue moving toward world levels, and domestic oil consumption is further replaced by consumption of domestic natural gas, the result could be more of an oil surplus for exports. It is difficult to project future inflows of workers' remittances and oil export earnings. We assume that total export earnings from goods and services will grow 3 to 4 percent a year in real terms in 1990-1995, and possibly faster after that.

Syria's near-term export prospects depend largely on the volume of oil production, since its base for exports is still narrow. Total non-oil exports reached $680 million, including exports of textiles of $270 million and exports of other manufactured goods of $160 million.[5] Net oil export earnings increased from low levels (even net imports) in earlier years, to $213 million in 1987 and $386 million in 1988. New oil field discoveries in recent years and declining domestic energy consumption (because of economic recession and rising oil prices) turned Syria into a modest net oil exporter in 1987. Crude oil production rose from 8 to 9 million tons in the 1970s to 10 million tons in 1986, 12 million tons in 1987, and nearly 14 million tons in 1988.[6] The production outlook was for further increases in crude oil production. The new oil fields produce a high-quality light crude. The old fields produce heavy high-sulfur crude, so it was necessary in the past to import light crudes to mix with domestic crude in the refineries. No crude was imported in 1988.

Export activities in Syria are undeveloped because of distortionary pricing policies and prolonged periods of inward-oriented development strategies. Merchandise exports represented a mere 6 percent of GNP in 1988, which is low compared with other economies of similar size and per capita income. Even Jordan's exports exceeded Syria's non-oil merchandise in recent years (table 2.6). Syria's exports are limited both in size and composition. Textiles account for 65 percent of total manufactured exports. Total non-oil exports shrank from $620 million a year in 1983-1984 to only $460 million a year in 1985-1986, recovering to an average $670 million in 1987-1988. The dip was attributable to a sharp drop in public non-oil exports—from $500 million in 1984 to $240 million in 1988—which was only partially compensated for by a spurt in private sector exports from an average annual $150 million in 1984-1985 to $440 million in 1988. As a result, private non-oil exports, which in 1988 represented 65 percent of the total, assumed a dominant role. The steady growth of private exports since 1986 was the result of government promotion policies designed to alleviate the shortage of foreign exchange. The government allowed some private exports to shift to more depreciated exchange rates. It also liberalized the export retention scheme, so that most private goods are actually exported at the free market rate. The policy-based boost in private exports suggests that exports could be expanded through adequate exchange rates and more liberal trade policies.

Growth prospect for Syrian exports in 1990-1995 and after depend primarily on growth in crude oil production (assuming only a moderate rise in oil prices) and further government promotion of private exports. Near-term diversification of exports could be stimulated by further removing structural and institutional rigidities and obstacles, extending the range of export categories by the private sector, and more frequent exchange rate adjustments to ensure profitability. Total non-oil merchandise exports, plus net oil exports have doubled, from a low of $550 million in 1983 to $1,070 million in 1988. Conceivably this source of revenue could double, to $2 billion in 1995, through vigorous export promotion policies.

In Jordan, phosphate rock, potash and fertilizers—mostly diamonium phosphate and phosphoric acid—made up almost 60 percent of the $874 million in domestic merchandise exports in 1988.[7] Total exports have risen in recent years—doubling between 1983 and 1988. This trend is largely attributable to the maturing in 1982 of large-scale development projects in potash recovery facilities and fertilizer production. There was also a marked increase in chemical, primarily pharmaceutical, exports—from $44 million in 1983 to $115 million in 1988. Exports of fruits and vegetables declined slightly, however, and those of other manufacturers—mainly construction materials and textiles—have stagnated since 1984. Food and manufactured exports, marketed largely in neighboring countries, were hurt by the regional recession.

Major investment programs aimed at increasing production of minerals and fertilizers are already under way or in an advanced planning stage. Their completion might increase the volume of exports, although prices could continue at current low levels in line with oil prices. The major markets for minerals and fertilizers are the Far East and Eastern Europe. Earning from these exports are projected to rise in the next few years, though probably not as fast as in 1983-1988. Whether Jordan's manufactured exports became more diversified depends on whether

Jordan broadens its narrow export base and penetrates new markets outside the region. Jordan's major export item is still labor services, although net remittances declined from a peak of $983 million in 1984 to $750 million in 1988. What happens to these transfers will determine to a great extent what happens to total current account income, of which they represent a large share. Prospects are not bright for a significant recovery in oil prices and for rapid economic expansion in the Gulf States in the near future. So, workers' remittances—and Jordan's other exports to the oil states—might continue to stagnate. It thus seems that only a moderate real rise in total exports of goods and services can be expected in the years ahead, before Jordan develops a broader base for diversified exports and reduces its overdependence on markets in the oil states.

SAVINGS, DEVELOPMENT NEEDS, AND INVESTMENT RATES

High rates of investment are a prerequisite for economic success. As a group, the developing countries with the fastest growing per capita incomes have had investment income ratios of about 20 to 25 percent. East Asian countries, which grew the fastest, had investment rates averaging about 30 to 35 percent. China invested roughly 33 percent of its GDP to achieve an annual growth rate of more than 9 percent in 1980-86. During the same period South Korea had an investment rate of 28 percent and a growth rate of more than 8 percent. Despite high average investment rates in Syria, Jordan, and Egypt (well over 20 percent in 1984-85) the average growth rates in all three countries were quite low (tables 1.4 and 2.5). Thus it seems that a minimum rate of investment is a necessary but not sufficient condition for sustained development. In two of the three countries, the resources devoted to fixed capital formation have dropped from very high levels to below 20 percent: in Syria from 29.6 percent in 1976-1980 to 16.6 percent in 1988, and in Egypt from 30.1 in 1982 to 19.3 in 1987 (table 9.2). In Jordan the investment rate fell from 50.5 percent in 1981 to 23.7 percent in 1988.

The three countries must return to higher investment rates to achieve sustained growth of 5 to 6 percent. The target rate for investment is different for each of the three countries, because it depends on the capital-output ratio. This can be demonstrated using the Harrod-Domar growth model. An open economy version of this model shows the equilibrium growth rate to be the ratio of the investment rate and the capital-output ratio. Increasing the investment rate equally in all three countries will produce different growth rates, since the capital-output ratios are different. A country with a higher capital-output ratio must increase the investment rate more to attain 5 to 6 percent growth. Such a big jump in the investment rate has negative implications for the balance of payments and for the countries' ability to absorb massive capital formation in a short time. Two mitigating elements can help restore equilibrium: first, to finance as much as possible new investments from domestic savings (discussed below), and second, to spread the investment process over a longer period. Absorption is a problem, as is any attempt to stretch a jump in the investment rate over time since it implies a slower rate of capital renewal and a lower growth rate.

Increases in the investment rate can be financed from domestic savings or from foreign resources. The domestic savings rate in Egypt, Jordan, and Syria is generally low and has declined dramatically in recent years. In Egypt, for example, it fell from about 15 percent in 1980 to roughly 8 percent in 1987 (table 9.3). In Jordan the savings rate has been negative since 1980, although improving recently.

Behind the drop in the Egyptian and Syrian savings rates was a drop in public savings, which were not only negative but declining. Reform was implemented in all three countries to reduce the budget deficit, which actually declined in recent years, but more must be done to increase public savings. To increase revenues, the tax system should be reformed (with a gradual shift from taxes on trade toward taxes on consumption and income). Fees should be much larger for the main users of such infrastructure and public utilities as water, drainage, sewerage, electricity, and telecommunications. More serious steps should be taken to control public spending, especially on defense and broad-based subsidies, and special efforts should be made to increase private savings.

In Syria, efforts to mobilize savings have been hampered by a rigid interest rate policy, low or negative public savings, and an overvalued exchange rate. The public savings rate has declined continuously since the mid-1970s and in 1983 became negative (-0.5 percent) falling to -5.4 percent in 1984 and -2.4 in 1985. (This trend was reversed the following year.) A cut in current public spending—including both

military spending and subsidies—produced substantial public savings in
1986-1988. Still, in 1987 the total savings rate declined to 9.9 percent,
the lowest level in a long time (table 9.3). The savings in the private
sector dropped significantly, from almost 19 percent of GDP in 1984 to
a mere 4 percent in 1987. For the first time, private savings were
insufficient to finance private investment. The causes of the drop in
savings are rooted in the interest and exchange rate policies for the last
decade. The high inflation rate and pronounced uncertainty may also
have caused a shift toward savings as the purchase of durable goods—a
type of saving that is not captured in the national accounts.
Conceivably, the sharp drop in private savings since 1984 could be the
result of measures taken to increase public savings—a phenomenon
observed in Israel and other economies where budget deficits were
reduced significantly.[8]

The structure and level of interest rates have remained unchanged
since 1981 despite sharply higher inflation rates and the lifting in 1988
of the 9 percent ceiling on interest rates. Current account deposits earn
only 4 percent for the private sector and 2 percent for the public sector;
6-month term deposits earn 7 percent and 12-month deposits 8 percent.
The highest rate of return on financial assets is the 9 percent paid on
investment certificates, which also have a lottery feature to promote
their sales. Consumer prices have risen at an average annual rate of 45
percent in 1986-1988,[9] so real interest rates are substantially negative.
This impedes the mobilization of resources and necessitates nonprice
rationing of loanable funds.

With interest rates so unattractive, time and savings deposits represent
a small part of the total money supply, averaging less than 12 percent
during the 1980s. More than 50 percent of the money supply in 1988
was currency, up from a stable lower level in 1983-1985. In the current
inflationary environment, Syria's public sector tries to hold its assets in
liquid form and in foreign currency. Foreign currency deposits
maintained in commercial banks doubled—to $264 million—between
the end of 1987 and June of 1988, following an early 1988 decision to
allow public sector enterprises to hold all of their export proceeds in
special foreign exchange accounts maintained in commercial banks.

Syria clearly needs a policy of flexible interest rates to promote
domestic bank savings and to discourage capital outflows. Now that the
legal ceiling on interest rates has been lifted, interest rates should be
raised immediately so that real interest rates will become positive.

The sharp drop in Egyptian savings is also partly attributable to negative real interest rates. Deposits earn, since May 1989, 12 percent for one-year maturity, and the rate for the three-month key deposits is only 8.5 percent. With inflation hovering around 25 percent, real interest rates are highly negative.[10] Moreover, Egyptians can hold assets in foreign currencies, which currently earn 7 to 8 percent in U.S. dollars. Egyptian currency is expected to be worth so little on the dollar that the difference between rates on domestic currency and foreign deposits is not enough to stimulate the holding of financial assets in domestic currency accounts. Foreign currency deposits increased from 25 percent of the money supply in 1985 to more than 40 percent by mid-1988. Such deposits also are invested abroad where they are unavailable to finance domestic capital formation or the balance of payments deficit.

Equally important, low interest rates have discouraged the transfer of remittances by Egyptian workers abroad—which is why Egyptians working abroad save at least $1 billion more a year than they transfer home. With more attractive interest and exchange rates, part of that sum could be recaptured.

The gross domestic savings rate does not reflect the savings from income nationals earn abroad and transfer home in the form of remittances. The difference between national and domestic savings is most dramatic in Jordan, where the domestic savings rate is negative and the national rate is positive—suggesting that Jordanians spend much more on consumption than they produce within their geographical boundaries. Net factor income from abroad had fallen sharply during the last three years, however, amounting to only 14.9 percent of GDP in 1987 compared with 26.7 percent in 1982. The net result has been a decline in the resources available for consumption and investment. Most of the adjustment came from a sharp drop in investment, which fell by almost 10 percent a year in 1983-1987 (table 9.3). Public consumption continued to grow during this period. Private consumption fell but not as much as investment did.

Savings trends in the three countries imply a resource gap of about 10 percent of GDP. Sustained growth requires an investment rate of 25 percent—which means a resource gap of 15 percent in Egypt, 30 percent in Jordan, and 12 percent in Syria. A higher savings rate is crucial to reverse negative economic trends, to strengthen the weak balance of payments, and to support essential investments.

Unfortunately the kinds of policy measures that can be used to encourage private savings are among the least well-known in economic policy. The level and structure of real interest rates are important but much more should be known about how to encourage private savings.

SOURCES OF EXTERNAL FINANCE: BRIDGING THE GAP

Predicting how much external finance will be available is a risky, even futile exercise, given the many uncertain factors that affect sources of foreign exchange. Table 9.4 shows the supply of external finance in certain years since 1980 and estimates of the average flow of funds for 1990-1995. The export figures assume an optimistic 25-percent real increase in Egyptian and Syrian exports and a 10-percent real increase for Jordan, where workers' remittances, which account for a large share of export earnings, are not expected to rise significantly. The projections of gross capital flows in table 9.4 are based mainly on the assumption that real oil prices will rise only moderately in the next decade, so there will be little change in the level of private transfers (workers' remittances), of aid, or of direct investment from the Arab oil countries.[11] Those projections also assume that U.S. grants and concessionary loans to Egypt will remain at current levels.

In all three countries, there is a large gap between projected annual needs for foreign exchange through 1995 and the expected flow of foreign resources to finance those needs. In Egypt, the gap is alarming—about $8 billion a year,[12] compared with $2 billion in 1987 (after rescheduling). Of course the projected gap reflects higher import levels—almost $6 billion higher than in 1987, but only $2.2 billion higher (in current prices) than in 1985. The absolute gap is smaller in Jordan and Syria—$800 million for Jordan and $1 billion for Syria—but significant in relation to GDP or export earnings. These are broad, not precise, estimates, but they signal future needs if sustained growth is to be maintained. Meanwhile, these gaps are annual averages for 1990-1995. If adjustment and reform programs produce three more efficient export-oriented economies, the gaps could shrink significantly later in the period.

To meet the Middle East's foreign exchange requirements, resource flows from external sources must increase during 1990-1995, but recently the trend has been for them to decline. In 1985-1986, gross capital inflows from all sources to Syria and Jordan were substantially lower in current prices than in 1980-1984. In Syria total net receipts declined from $1,750 million in 1980 to just over $700 million in 1985 and 1986. In Jordan total net receipts dropped even more: from $1,550 million in 1980 to just over $350 million in 1985-1986. Receipts declined in both countries because of a decline in concessional flows, particularly from Arab oil countries. Organization of Arab Petroleum Exporting Countries (OAPEC) assistance to Syria fell from $1,600 million in 1979-1981 to $530 million in 1988; assistance to Jordan fell from $1,200 million to $560 million in the same period (table 2.3). Both countries depend heavily on OAPEC countries for foreign assistance. In Syria they provided 94 percent of such assistance in 1980 and 82 percent in 1985; in Jordan, they provided 73 percent in 1980 and in 1985 such aid was even higher than total net receipts (table 9.3). The picture is somewhat different in Egypt, where most net foreign receipts come from the Western world. Foreign receipts peaked at $3,200 million in 1982 then declined to their 1987 level of $2,500 million.[13] Most of that drop is attributable to the decline in exports (mainly of oil and workers' remittances) from a peak of $6,700 million in 1985 to $4,000 million in 1987.

The projected gap between foreign exchange needs and supplies is wide for all three countries. How much capital flows can increase depends on trends in Arab aid and on whether the three countries adopt needed reforms with reasonable speed. Given the severe debt service problem in Egypt and Jordan, it is unrealistic to expect that a reform program, however tough and speedy, will immediately reestablish their creditworthiness and extricate them from debt. Emergency action should be taken by these countries and their creditors, donors, and multilateral international organizations. Surely there is a place for further debt relief for Egypt and Jordan and more concessional flow.

The objective of economic independence is still distant. Advancing toward it requires immense efforts and sacrifices, but it is not inaccessible. The finance gap could be reduced through prolonged recessions and reduced imports, but this would not improve living conditions. The alternative—reducing the gap through a growth-oriented strategy—requires extra external finance and debt relief. The SDF could help bridge the gap, which should contract in the medium term.

Resolving the Debt Crisis

Resolving the debt crisis in Egypt and Jordan does not mean eliminating debt. Not only must both countries continue borrowing to finance growth and development, but borrowing is economically rational. Avoiding a debt problem means keeping debt at such a level that the country can service it from current and future trade flows. "Sustainable debt" means there is confidence that the country can service its debt over time, under a reasonable range of economic conditions. There might be short periods of heavy borrowing, but the ratio of debt to real per capita output should generally decline or remain steady.

To ensure that debt does not threaten the political stability of Egypt and Jordan, the debt-service burden should not prevent them from escaping from economic stagnancy. But to guarantee their financial stability and creditworthiness, financial flows to the two countries should be directed at the investments with the greatest promise of return—with minimal pressure for more protection of either domestic goods or financial markets.

Approaches to resolving the debt crisis should also be efficient in terms of stimulating investment and thus economic growth. Solutions must be presented in the context of overall reform of domestic policies at both the macroeconomic level (especially fiscal restraint and sound management of exchange rates) and the microeconomic level (including liberalized markets, removal of distortions, and so on).

The need for structural policy reform in Egypt, Jordan, Syria, and other debtor countries is a consistent theme in most analyses of the debt crises. The Baker plan, for example—which was announced by then U.S. Treasury Secretary James A. Baker in September 1985 and has formed the nucleus of debt policy since then—recommended broad reform as a precondition for access to new funds.[14] The IMF has long recommended that Egypt, Syria, and Jordan adopt responsible domestic policies. Others believe policy reform to be the critical element in resolving the debt crisis.[15] According to A.O. Krueger, "Longer-term resolution of the problem requires first and foremost a realignment of domestic policies to achieve greater productivity from existing resources and higher returns from resource accumulation."[16] Despite widespread support for policy reform, its implementation in Egypt, Syria, and Jordan faces several hurdles. First, reform often means substantially reducing consumption, which would be hard to swallow in countries where consumption has declined for most of the last decade. Second, the costs of reform often fall on lower income groups. Third, the size of the debt overhang can act as a tax on policy reform. The cost of structural adjustment falls on the debtor. Benefits—particularly the greater capacity to service debt—if they accrue largely to creditors, may be viewed by these Middle Eastern countries as a disincentive to reform.

Partial debt forgiveness may counteract this disincentive. Debt forgiveness, which can be applied to principal or interest, is a key element in debt resolution plans such as those by Bradley[17] and Sachs[18] which build on the Baker framework. These plans suggest providing outright debt relief, especially for countries that experienced a fall in GNP. To date, the most wide-ranging proposal for mandatory debt forgiveness is the recommendation of the United Nations Conference on Trade and Development for an across-the-board 30 percent write-down of commercial bank debt. In return, the debtor countries would be required to allocate all interest saved to investment in export industries. Debt forgiveness would be attractive to the debtor countries because it would reduce foreigners' claims on domestic resources if events were to become favorable and their ability to service debt to rise.[19]

In earlier chapters we concluded that debt reduction and adjustment policy in Egypt, Jordan, and Syria cannot be generated by market forces, which are currently limited. The alternative is government intervention and the commitment of international, bilateral, and multilateral public funds. What is important is quick relief through official intervention. One mechanism to facilitate a solution would be a new international institution, such as the SDF with the aim of supporting reforms and adjustments discussed in this book.

It may seem ironic to conclude this book by recommending massive aid to these three countries, when we have shown how an abundance of aid in the decade of prosperity did not build a more prosperous future and is responsible for the countries' current economic misery. The recommendations for more aid to this troubled area of the world must be understood in the context of conditionality, policy reform, and structural change. Only well-targeted aid and new loans can turn these economies around, create a better future, and justify the mortgage that future generations will have to repay. The fruits of this investment should make it easier to repay the debts.

NOTES

1. World Bank 1989e, p. 559.
2. Ibid., p. 347.
3. Several important initiatives have been taken in recent years to provide debt relief, in the form of debt rescheduling or real debt reduction schemes.
4. Unofficial estimates of Syria's military debt to the Soviet Union range from $10 to $15 billion. There are signs that the Soviet Union's demanding that Syria begin making payments on it. See *Financial Times* 1989.
5. Plus $60 million for phosphates and $30 million for unclassified exports.
6. According to preliminary figures crude oil production increased to 16 million tons in 1989. *Petroleum Economist* January 1990, p. 27.
7. Net of re-exports, primarily to Iraq.
8. Bank of Israel 1988, figure 2.3, p. 31.
9. Retail price indices in Damascus (Syria, Central Bureau of Statistics).
10. The highest rate is 16 percent, for seven-year deposits.
11. Although oil export earnings could increase somewhat as export volumes increase.
12. About $2.5 billion a year excluding debt service payments. The current account deficit is estimated to reach $5.5 billion (excluding interest payments but including private transfers and official grants).
13. Excluding U.S. military grants of $1.3 billion annually.
14. Wertmen 1987.
15. Sengupta 1988.
16. Krueger 1988.
17. Bradley 1986.
18. Sachs 1986.
19. Krugman 1988.

Table 9.1 Foreign Exchange Payments, 1990-1995
(millions of U.S. dollars)

	1982	1983	1985	1987	1990-1995 Projected annual average
Egypt					
Imports of goods and services (excluding interest)	13,299	13,746	17,267	13,878	19,621
Debt service payments	1,887	2,213	2,280	1,734	5,600
Total	15,186	15,959	19,547	15,612	25,221
Jordan					
Imports of goods and services (excluding interest)	4,517.7	4,143.0	4,017.0	3,976.0	4,500
Debt service payments	176.5	210.1	351.0	734.2	1,000
Total	4,694.2	4,353.1	4,368.0	4,493.0	5,500
Syria					
Imports of goods and services (excluding interest)	4,583.6	5,190.0	4,668.0	3,710.0	5,000
Debt service payments	303.8	304.4	297.2	365.0	540
Total	4,887.4	5,494.4	4,965.2	4,075.0	5,540

Source: The World Bank, 1989e.

Table 9.2 Investment and Savings Ratios

	Jordan		Egypt		Syria	
	Investment ratio	Savings ratio	Investment ratio	Savings ratio	Investment ratio	Savings ratio
1980	41.1	-9.0	27.5	15.2	27.5	10.3
1981	50.5	-15.0	29.5	14.1	23.1	13.9
1982	46.9	-17.0	30.1	15.2	23.7	12.6
1983	35.8	-19.2	28.7	17.7	23.6	11.9
1984	32.4	-16.8	27.5	14.0	23.7	13.3
1985	30.5	-15.7	26.7	14.5	23.7	12.0
1986	29.6	-8.6	23.7	13.8	23.2	13.3
1987	26.4	-5.1	19.3	8.4	18.6	9.9
1988	23.7	—	—	—	16.6	—

Note: The investment ratio is the ratio of gross domestic investment gross domestic product (GDP). The savings ratio is the ratio of gross domestic savings to GDP. In Jordan, gross domestic savings are always negative, yielding a negative savings ratio.

Table 9.3 Servicing the External Debt
(millions of current U.S. dollars)

	1980	1981	1982	1983	1984	1985	1986	1987
Egypt								
Repayments	1,075	1,361	1,492	1,548	1,504	1,536	1,180	928
Interest	456	658	618	665	746	744	768	806
Debt service as share of exports of goods and services	18.7	24.0	25.3	24.9	23.5	23.4	22.2	26.5
Jordan								
Repayments	75.7	135.3	135.0	110.6	123.0	211.0	237.0	334
Interest	57.6	66.4	62.1	99.5	88.9	140.0	152.0	183
Debt service as share of exports of goods and services	7.5	9.7	10.3	9.8	16.1	19.2	21.8	
Syria								
Repayments	220.5	243.5	242.4	231.5	201.0	217.7	10.5	253.0
Interest	76.9	55.2	72.9	72.9	77.4	79.5	86.5	112.0
Debt service as share of exports of goods and services	11.6	10.6	12.2	11.2	10.8	14.8	15.6	16.5

Source: The World Bank, 1989e.

149

Table 9.4 Supply of External Finance, Egypt
(millions of U.S. dollars)

	1982	1983	1985	1987	1990-1995[a]
Exports of goods and services	8,430	8,870	9,754	8,061	10,076
Gross capital flows					
Official grants	395	675	1,171	1,052	1,100
Private transfers	1,935	3,165	3,496	2,845	3,000
Concessional loans	1,464	1,172	1,098	959	1,000
Nonconcessional loans (net)	45	289	-214	-852	300
Direct investment	885	966	1,289	869	1,000
Supplier credit	1,050	1,120	850	645	700
Total	14,204	16,257	17,444	13,579	17,176

a. Projected annual average.
Sources: The World Bank, 1989e, and the International Monetary Fund, International Financial Statistics.

Table 9.4 Supply of External Finance, Jordan
(millions of U.S. dollars)

	1982	1983	1985	1987	1990-1995[a]
Exports of goods and services	2,208.9	2,042.2	2,181.7	2,376.4	2,600
Gross capital flows					
Official grants	1,032.0	798.0	739.0	566.0	800
Private transfers	975.5	910.0	921.1	742.9	750
Loans	479.9	508.0	528.0	349.1	400
Direct investment	56.0	30.1	25.7	38.3	50
Other loans and supplier credit (*net*)	-276.4	104.2	-306.0	160.6	100
Total	4,503.9	4,407.2	4,426.0	4,255.7	4,700

a. Projected annual average.
Sources: The World Bank, 1989e, and the International Monetary Fund, International Financial Statistics.

151

Table 9.4 Supply of External Finance, Syria
(millions of U.S. dollars)

	1982	1983	1985	1987	1990-1995[a]
Exports of goods and services	2,821.1	2,708.8	2,440.4	2,207.0	2,750
Gross capital flows					
Official grants	1,398.0	1,304.0	1,090.0	769.0	900
Private transfers	581.7	461.1	293.0	250.0	300
Loans	369.3	320.7	478.3	540.3	350
Direct investment	—	—	—	—	—
Other loans and supplier credit (net)	—	—	—	—	—

a. Projected annual average.
Sources: The World Bank, 1989e, and the International Monetary Fund, International Financial Statistics.

REFERENCES

Benoit, Emil. 1978. "Growth and Defense Spending in Developing Countries." *Economic Development and Cultural Change* 26:

Bank of Israel. 1988. *Annual Report 1987*. Jerusalem.

Bank of Israel, 1989. *Annual Report 1988*. Jerusalem.

Bradley, B. 1986. "A Proposal for Third World Debt Management." Speech delivered in Zurich, June 29.

Corden, W. Max. 1988. "Debt Relief and Adjustment Incentives." *Staff Paper, International Monetary Fund* 35: 401-21.

————. 1988. "International Debt Facility." *Staff Paper, International Monetary Fund* 35: 401-21

Corden, W. Max and Peter Neary. 1982. "Booming Sector and Deindustrialization in a Small Open Economy." *Economic Journal* 92: 825-48.

Deger, Sadet. 1986. *Military Expenditure in Third World Countries: The Economic Effects*. London: Routledge, Kegan & Paul.

The Economist. January 20, 1990.

Egypt, various issues. Central Bank of Egypt. *Economic Review*, Cairo.

Egypt, various issues. *Monthly Bulletin of Foreign Trade*, Central Agency for Public Mobilization and Statistics, Cairo.

Financial Times. "De Facto Disarmament." September 4, 1989.

Gelb, Alan. 1988. *Oil Windfalls: Blessing or Curse?* New York: Oxford University Press.

International Monetary Fund (IMF). Various years. *International Financial Statistics*. Washington, D.C.

————. 1988. *Egypt: Recent Economic Development*. Washington, D.C.

————. 1988. *Jordan: Recent Economic Development*. Washington, D.C.

————. 1988. *Syria: Recent Economic Development.* Washington, D.C.

————. 1989. *Egypt: Recent Economic Development.* Washington, D.C.

————. 1989. *Jordan: Recent Economic Development.* Washington, D.C.

————. 1989. *Syria: Recent Economic Development.* Washington, D.C.

Krueger, Anne O. April 1980. "Resolving the Debt Crisis and Restoring Developing Countries' Creditworthiness." Paper prepared for Carnegie Rochester Conference. North Holland Publishing Company, forthcoming.

Krugman, Paul. 1988. "Financing vs. Forgiving a Debt Overhang." National Bureau of Economic Research (NBER) Working Paper 2486. Cambridge, Mass.: National Bureau of Economic Research.

————. 1988. "Market-based Debt Reduction Schemes." NBER Working Paper 2587. Cambridge, Mass.: National Bureau of Economic Research.

Lavy, Victor. 1983. "The Welfare and Transfer Effects of Cotton Price Policies in Egypt, 1965-1978." *American Journal of Agricultural Economics.* August 1983, pp. 576-582

————. 1984. "The Productivity of Foreign Aid in a Developing Economy: Egypt." *Journal of Developing Areas.* September 1984.

————. 1985. "Cropping Pattern, Mechanization, Child Labor, and Fertility Behavior in Rural Egypt." *Economic Development and Cultural Change.* July 1985, pp. 777-792.

————. 1986. "Determinants of Fertility Cycles in Rural Egypt: Behavioral and Biological Linkages." *Demography.* February 1986, pp. 13-30.

————. 1986. "The Distributional Impact of Economic Growth and Decline in Egypt." *Middle Eastern Studies.* January 1986, pp. 89-103.

————. 1990. "Egypt and Syria's Journey Through Socialism: A Forty-year Perspective." in *Wealth of Nations in the Twentieth Century.* Ramon H. Myers, editor. Stanford University Press, forthcoming.

Petroleum Economist. January 1990.

Sachs, Jeffrey. 1986. "Managing the LDC Dept Crisis." Brookings Paper on Economic Activity, pp. 397-440.

Sengupta, A.K. "Remedy for Debt Overhang." *The International Economy.* July-August 1988.

Shahar, Ben, Gideon Fishelson, and Zaer Hirs. 1989. *Economic Cooperation and Middle East Peace.* London: Weidenfeld and Nicholson.

Sheffer, Eliezer. 1984. "The Economic Burden of the Arms Race Between the Confrontation States and Israel." In Zvi Lanir, ed., *Israeli Security Planning in the 1980s.* New York: Praeger.

Syria. various issues. Central Bank of Syria, Reseach Department. *Quarterly Bulletin,* Damascus.

————. various issues. Central Bureau of Statistics. *Summary of Foreign Trade,* Damascus.

van Wijnbergen, Sweden. 1984. "The 'Dutch Disease': A Disease After All?" *The Economic Journal.* March 94: 41-55.

Wertmen, Paul. 1987. "The Baker Plan: A Remedy for International Debt Crisis." Washington, D.C.: Library of Congress, Congressional Research Service.

World Bank. 1987a. *World Development Report 1987.* New York: Oxford University Press.

———. 1987b. "Egypt: Review of the Finances of the Decentralized Public Sector." World Bank Report No. 6421-EGT. March 1987. Washington, D.C.

———. 1988a. *Annual Report.* Washington, D.C.

———. 1988b. *World Bank Atlas.* Washington, D.C.

———. 1989a. *Social Indicators of Development.* Washington, D.C.

———. 1989b. *Trends in Developing Economies.* Washington, D.C.

———. 1989c. *World Development Indicators.* Washington, D.C.

———. 1989d. *World Development Report 1989.* New York: Oxford University Press.

———. 1989e. *World Tables 1988-89.* Washington, D.C.

U.S. Arms Control and Disarmament Agency (ACDA). 1987a. *ACDA 1987 Report.* Washington, D.C.

———. 1987b. *World Military Expenditures Tables 1987.* Washington, D.C.

———. 1988. "World Military Expenditures and Arms Transfers 1987." Washington, D.C.

INDEX

(Page numbers in italics indicate material in tables.)

About the Authors

VICTOR LAVY and ELIEZER SHEFFER are both professors of economics at Hebrew University.